Media, Religion and Culture

Religion has always been shaped by the media of its time, and today we live in a media culture that informs much of what we think and how we behave. Religious believers, communities and institutions use media as tools to communicate, but also as locations where they construct and express identity, practice religion, and build community.

This lively book offers a comprehensive introduction to the contemporary field of religion, media, and culture. It explores:

- the religious content of media texts and the reception of those texts by religious consumers who appropriate and reuse them in their own religious work;
- how new forms of media provide fresh locations within which new religious voices emerge, people reimagine the "task" of religion, and develop and perform religious identity.

Jeffrey H. Mahan includes case study examples from both established and new religions and each chapter is followed by insightful reflections from leading scholars in the field. Illustrated throughout, the book also contains a glossary of key terms, discussion questions, and suggestions for further reading.

Jeffrey H. Mahan holds the Ralph E. and Norma E. Peck Chair in Religion and Public Communication and is Professor of Ministry, Media and Culture at Iliff School of Theology in Denver, USA. He is affiliate faculty at the Center for Media, Religion and Culture at the University of Colorado in Boulder and co-editor with Bruce David Forbes of *Religion and Popular Culture in America*.

D1446057

Media, Religion and Culture

An introduction

Jeffrey H. Mahan

Routledge
Taylor & Francis Group

LONDON AND NEW YORK

First published in 2014
by Routledge
2 Park Square, Milton Park, Abingdon, Oxon OX14 4RN

and by Routledge
711 Third Avenue, New York, NY 10017

Routledge is an imprint of the Taylor & Francis Group, an informa business

© 2014 Jeffrey H. Mahan for main chapters; individual contributors, their contributions

The right of the authors to be identified for their chapters has been asserted in accordance with sections 77 and 78 of the Copyright, Designs and Patents Act 1988.

All rights reserved. No part of this book may be reprinted or reproduced or utilised in any form or by any electronic, mechanical, or other means, now known or hereafter invented, including photocopying and recording, or in any information storage or retrieval system, without permission in writing from the publishers.

Trademark notice: Product or corporate names may be trademarks or registered trademarks, and are used only for identification and explanation without intent to infringe.

British Library Cataloguing in Publication Data
A catalogue record for this book is available from the British Library

Library of Congress Cataloging in Publication Data
Mahan, Jeffrey H.
Media, religion, and culture : an introduction / Jeffrey H. Mahan.
Includes bibliographical references.
1. Mass media in religion. 2. Mass media--Religious aspects. 3. Religion and culture. I. Title.
BL638.M34 2014
201'.7--dc23
2013043417

ISBN: 978-0-415-68318-0 (hbk)
ISBN: 978-0-415-68320-3 (pbk)
ISBN: 978-1-315-77706-1 (ebk)

Typeset in Bembo
by Taylor & Francis Books

For Louise

Contents

Figures

Contributors

Heidi A. Campbell is Associate Professor of Communication at Texas A&M University. Dr. Campbell's recent books include *When Religion Meets New Media* (2010) and *Digital Religion: Understanding Religious Practice in New Media Worlds* (2013). She is the founder of the Network for New Media, Religion and Digital Culture Studies.

Grace Chiou is a Doctoral student in Religious Studies at University of Denver-Iliff School of Theology, CO. Chiou is co-author with Dr. Lynn Schofield Clark of "Feminist orientations in the methodologies of the media, religion, and culture field," which appeared in *Media, Religion and Gender*, Mia Lövheim, ed. (2013). Chiou has presented her work at the International Society for Media, Religion and Culture's Religion in the Rocky Mountains and Great Plains Conference, the American Studies Conference, and the NYU Neil Postman Graduate Conference.

Dan Clanton is Assistant Professor of Religious Studies at Doane College, NE. Dr. Clanton's publications include: *Understanding Religion and Popular Culture* (edited with Terry Ray Clark, 2012) and *The End Will Be Graphic: Apocalyptic in Comic Books and Graphic Novels* (edited, 2012).

Lynn Schofield Clark is Professor of Media, Film, and Journalism Studies at University of Denver, CO. Dr. Schofield Clark is the Director of the Estlow International Center for Journalism and New Media at the University of Denver, where she teaches participatory courses in media and culture as well as in qualitative research methods. Clark is author of *The Parent App: Understanding Families in a Digital Age* (2012) and *From Angels to Aliens: Teenagers, the Media, and the Supernatural* (2005), co-author of *Media, Home, and Family* (2004), editor of *Religion, Media, and the Marketplace* (2007), and co-editor of *Practicing Religion in the Age of the Media* (2002). She is the Founding VP of the International Society for Media, Religion, and Culture.

Nabil Echchaibi is Assistant Professor of Journalism and Communication at University of Colorado, Boulder. Dr. Echchaibi is Associate Director of the Center for Media, Religion, and Culture and specializes in identity politics among young Muslims in the Arab world and in diaspora. His work on diasporic media and the massification of religious authority through the proliferation of Islamic media has appeared in various international publications. Books include *Voicing Diasporas: Ethnic Radio in Paris and Berlin between Cultures and Renewal* (2011), and he is at work on *Formation of the Muslim Modern: Islam, Media and Alternative Modernity*.

Michael Hemenway is Director of Academic and Information Technology at Iliff School of Theology, CO. He is Technology Consultant to the Nida Institute for Biblical Scholarship. Hemenway is also working toward his doctorate in Religious Studies in the University of Denver-Iliff School of Theology joint PhD program. His research focuses on the relationship between book technology and religious identity.

Kathryn Lofton is Professor of Religious Studies, American Studies, History, and Divinity at Yale University, CT. Dr. Lofton is the author of *Oprah: The Gospel of an Idea* (2011). She is currently working on several projects, including a study of sexuality and Protestant fundamentalism; an analysis of the culture concept of the Goldman Sachs Group; and a religious history of Bob Dylan.

David Morgan is Professor of Religion and Art, Art History and Visual Studies at Duke University, NC. Dr. Morgan publishes on the history of religious visual culture, art history, critical theory, and religion and media. Recent books include *The Embodied Eye: Religious Visual Culture and the Social Life of Feeling* (2012) and *The Lure of Images: A History of Religion and Visual Media in America* (2007). He edited and contributed to: *Religion and Material Culture: The Matter of Belief* (2010) and *Key Words in Religion, Media, and Culture* (2008). Morgan is co-founder of the journal *Material Religion*, and co-editor of a book series at Routledge entitled Routledge Research in Religion, Media and Culture.

Sarah M. Pike is Professor of Comparative Religion at California State University, Chico. Dr. Pike is the author of *Earthly Bodies, Magical Selves: Contemporary Pagans and the Search for Community* (2001) and *New Age and Neopagan Religions in America* (2004) and has written numerous articles, book chapters, and encyclopedia articles on contemporary Paganism, the New Age movement, the Burning Man festival, new religions in the media, environmentalism, and youth culture. She is also Director of the Chico Humanities Center.

S. Brent Plate is Visiting Associate Professor of Religious Studies at Hamilton College, NY. Dr. Plate is co-founder of *Material Religion: The Journal of Objects, Art, and Belief* and serves on the editorial committee of the American Academy of Religion. His books include *A History of Religion in 5½ Objects* (forthcoming), *Religion and Film* (2009), and *Blasphemy: Art That Offends* (2006).

Sophia Shafi is Visiting Assistant Professor of Islamic Studies at Iliff School of Theology, CO. Dr. Shafi writes on a number of subjects related to Islam, including pilgrimage traditions and architecture, the image of the harem as a den of monsters in colonial literature and Hollywood film, and the trope of Turning Turk in Hollywood film and television. She has presented papers at academic conferences, at the Metropolitan Museum of Art, University of Chicago, and Indiana University, among other places. Her book *Muslim Monsters in the Western Imagination* is forthcoming in 2014.

Jeremy Stolow is Associate Professor of Communication Studies at Concordia University, Montreal. Dr. Stolow is the author of *Orthodox By Design* (2010) and *Deus in Machina* (2013). He is also a member of the International Advisory Board of the Center for Religion and Media (New York University) and the Centre de recherche sur l'intermédialité (Université de Montréal).

Benjamin Thevenin is Assistant Professor of Media Arts at Brigham Young University (BYU), UT. A scholar and film maker, Dr. Thevenin received an award from the National Association for Media Literacy for "The Re-Politicization of Media Literacy Education." He serves as Director of BYU's "Hands on a Camera project: a media literacy initiative for youth."

Rachel Wagner is Associate Professor of Religion at Ithaca College, NY. Dr. Wagner publishes in the areas of religion and media, religion and film, and religion and video games. Publications include: *Godwired: Religion, Ritual and Virtual Reality* (2011) and chapters in *Understanding Religion and Popular Culture* (2012); *The Encyclopedia of Video Games, Digital Religion* (2012); and *Playing Games with God* (forthcoming). She is Co-Chair of the Religion, Film and Visual Culture Group of the American Academy of Religion.

Pete Ward is Professor of Theology and Ministry at King's College, London. Dr. Ward's publications include *Gods Behaving Badly: Media, Religion and Celebrity Culture* (2011) and *Participation and Mediation: A Practical Theology for the Liquid Church* (2008).

Deborah Whitehead is Assistant Professor of Religious Studies at University of Colorado, Boulder. Dr. Whitehead is Co-Chair of the Women and Religion Section at the American Academy of Religion and the author of several articles as well as two forthcoming books, one on William James and American pragmatism, and the other on contemporary US evangelicals and mediation.

Foreword

This book represents a watershed in the development of scholarship on media and religion. For many years now, scholars, professionals, and observers from a variety of disciplines have been turning their attention to the traditionally overlooked intersection between religion and media. All religions have of course always been mediated. Music, dance, images, texts, talismans, narratives, dramas, all of these and more have been ways that "the religious" has been expressed, codified, circulated, critiqued, consumed, embodied, understood, taught, reconsidered, and struggled against. Thus there should have been nothing new with the emergence of new mediations of religion in relation to new forms of media. But the industrial media of the mass-press era, and later the electric media and electronic media of the so-called "media age," seemed to be of a different order.

Religion and media have long been thought of as separate and distinct spheres (a division that is increasingly difficult to maintain either practically or rhetorically). The emergence of ever newer and seemingly revolutionary media seemed to confront the authenticity and purity of religion. Thus, when the new form that we now call "Televangelism" emerged in the West late in the last century, it was seen to be a revolutionary break. Attention was focused on what observers and scholars alike saw to be a new evolution in religious practice. And of course it was new, but we can see today that it was only one example of the ways in which what we think of as fundamentally "religious" is being remade through its interaction with media. This happened with the printing press and probably happened with stone tablets as well. Religions have always been transformed by their mediation, and we should have been able to see that.

But many couldn't initially see that, with much attention focused on how the particular institutions and structures and practices of the media were affecting particular structures and practices in religion. We can now see how that was only part of the story. The more profound story is in how mediation in fact is integral to religion and to senses and practices of "the religious," "the spiritual," and the whole range of things that bear a family resemblance to those senses and practices.

Taking this perspective means that those who want to understand media and religion have had to think in new ways. We have had to think very differently about popular practice and popular culture. In the past, it was convenient to dismiss popular forms of religious practice as marginal, trivial, or inconsequential. Today we can see that contemporary forms of media and mediation have moved "the popular" to the center of religious meaning and articulation. We have had to think differently about authority. In the past, we were able to critique many mediations of religion through the lens of religious authority and its ability to legitimate or value certain symbols, truth claims, icons, and practices. Today we see that emergent religious practices in and through emergent media are providing a vibrant challenge to traditional religious institutions and authorities, and are even making new forms and contexts of authority.

We have also had to rethink our definitions of "media" or of "communication." It used to be that media or communication were mostly considered important to religion to the extent that they could be used to promote or extend specific religions or religious movements. Today we can see that the processes of mediation and communication are at the center of religious meaning, practice, and evolution, and that their logics actually determine what it is possible for religious or spiritual impulses, practices, networks, and movements to be or to achieve. The logics of media, including visuality, mediatic invocation of sensation in addition to rationality, their various esthetic forms, and the positions, affordances, and subjectivities into which they hail their various practitioners ("producers," "consumers," and "pro-sumers"), are the abiding logics today. Traditional ways of structuring "the religious" or "the spiritual" are challenged. And they are largely challenged by *practice*, which is a fundamental logic of mediated religion today.

All of this rethinking has been made possible by the emergence, across disciplines, of a community or a network of scholars and practitioners focused on the intersection between "media" and "religion." They have come from the fields of communication, media studies, religion, film studies, anthropology, art history, folklore, geography, history, sociology, marketing, ethnomusicology, law, and more. Each of them seems to have begun the same way. First, there was a recognition that settled theory was not taking into account the ways that the mediation of religion is responsible for the evolution of religion. Then there was the sense of being quite alone in noticing this, and looking for intellectual or other resources or networks or colleagues who might be interested. If they persevered, they found colleagues—typically in disciplines beyond their own—who shared these insights and interests, and gradually communities of scholarship formed both within disciplines and beyond them.

That has been one of the most interesting, exciting, and productive things about the field of media and religion. Its cross-disciplinarity has been its greatest strength, and has profoundly extended its reach, significance, and influence. This cross-disciplinarity is obvious in these pages, which present the outlines of this field as it appears today. It is a watershed, as I said, as the first such book to be produced. But it is also a stock-taking and an assessment of where the scholarly discourse of media and religion stands and what it has learned and achieved. This is not to say that any of this is by any means settled. There is much, much more to be done to deepen and extend the insights represented here.

This book does represent the dimensions I've raised. One can see within it the traces of evolving thinking about media and religion and struggles over how best to study their intersection. It also represents the cross-disciplinarity that has been so essential to progress.

But, it also represents one thing that I think we can recognize as an irreversible accomplishment along the historical path I've outlined. Earlier generations of students and scholars had to struggle to find resources and insights and support for their interest in media and religion. Many felt alone and isolated. Jeffrey Mahan has, through this fine work, confirmed the existence of this field of inquiry, has demonstrated its breadth, depth, and interdisciplinarity, and has produced a volume that is an essential foundation for its further growth and development.

Stewart M. Hoover
Center for Media, Religion and Culture,
University of Colorado at Boulder

Acknowledgments

Books are never the sole work of the person whose name appears on the cover. More than 30 years ago my graduate school professors: Gerald Forshey, Richard Tholin, and Stuart Kaminsky at Garrett-Evangelical Theological School and Northwestern University encouraged my early interest in religion, film, and popular culture and my intellectual debts start there. Through their work and conversation, colleagues in the International Society for Media, Religion, and Culture have shaped my thinking. Stewart Hoover, David Morgan, and Jolyon Mitchell, the editors of the Routledge Research in Religion, Media and Culture series, first asked me to take on this project and provided important feedback at early stages. Special thanks are due to the colleagues named later in this volume who provided the brief sample reflections based on their own work which illustrate the chapters. Katherine Ong at Routledge has been helpful, encouraging, and persistent with a book that has missed several deadlines, and which might still be in process without her support.

Routledge acknowledges that some material in the introduction and Part 1 draws upon an earlier article by the same author: Mahan, J. H. (2012), "Religion and Media," *Religion Compass*, 6: 14–25, doi: 10.1111/j.1749–8171.2011.00330.x, reproduced by kind permission of Wiley-Blackwell. Routledge gives Jeffrey H. Mahan proper credit as the original author of this article. Portions of Chapters 4 and 5 were presented at the 2012 meeting of the International Society for Media, Religion, and Culture at Eskisehir, Turkey. Thanks to the colleagues there who commented and responded to the presentation.

Iliff School of Theology provided a crucial sabbatical leave during which the first ideas for the book emerged, and a later research leave which enabled writing. The Joint PhD program in Religious Studies of Iliff and the University of Denver assigned research assistants at several stages. The doctoral student assistants: Grace Chiou, Ryan Hall, and Tim Sakelos were conversation partners and contributed generously of their time and intellectual energy. Rodolfo J. Hernández-Díaz in Iliff School of Theology's IT department consulted about computer mysteries, laid hands on the laptop when it was needed, and cleaned up the final manuscripts.

Friends and colleagues including Ted Vial, William Dean, Roger Cauthon, Rabbi Adam Morris, and the students in my online course on media, religion, and culture read and responded to portions of the manuscript. My son, the composer Jason Hoogerhyde, helped me think through the discussion of sound, speech, and music. Finally, my spouse, The Rev. Louise Mahan, has been a conversation partner, a proofreader, and a source of encouragement throughout. The failings of the volume are my own, but its contributions are due in no small measure to the challenge, support, and encouragement of these and others for which I am deeply grateful.

Jeffrey H. Mahan
Iliff School of Theology

Part 1

Religious identity in media cultures

Noting the decline of once-dominant religious traditions and the rise of a see-mingly more secular way of life, particularly in the public square, some people have suggested that religion would disappear from modern society. But this has not happened. Religion remains vital and active, though sometimes in new and unexpected ways. The religious task is increasingly understood as a matter of crafting an individual identity rather than adopting a community identity, and this often happens in less fixed and institutionalized spaces. Traditional centers of religious authority are challenged by the contemporary media culture.

Chapter 1: Relating media, religion, and culture makes the case for why we ought to think about media, religion, and culture in relationship to each other, particularly in what has been called late-modernity. It provides an overview of the assumptions that shape the book and introduces and defines key terms.

Chapter 2: Making and articulating religious identity looks at how religious belief and practice change over time, how traditional centers of religious authority are challenged by the assumptions of contemporary media culture, and how people draw on multiple religious traditions and from apparently secular popular culture to craft and enact complex religious identities.

Chapter 3: Believing and practicing in a digital world considers the way that religion moves into new media spaces, and how the technical and social possibilities of digital culture lend themselves to new understandings of religious identity and authority.

1 Relating media, religion, and culture

Key ideas

- Religion, media, and culture should be understood in relationship to each other.
- *Religion* refers to a complex variety of beliefs and practices, and provides a way for us to understand cultural activity such as fandom that may not immediately seem religious.
- Particular *media cultures* emerge around new forms of mediation. People and their religions are shaped by their media cultures and adopt the forms and assumptions of that media culture. This makes media change a difficult cross-cultural project for many individuals and societies.
- Digital media are creating new spaces for religious experimentation, and people and religious institutions and communities rooted in early forms of media find this challenging.

In the vocabulary of the Internet a *hyperlink* is a highlighted term within a text where a mouse click connects you to some other crucial and related data, making it easy to move back and forth between the sites. The presentation of "media," "religion," and "culture" as a coherent area of study is based on the assumption that they have such a crucial connection to each other that, to understand any one of these concepts, we have to see it in relationship to the other two. They are intellectually hyperlinked. Thus, for example, to best understand and describe religion, we see it in relationship to media and culture, leaping back and forth between the concepts. Further, the concepts and their relationships are not fixed. *Media, Religion and Culture* explores the idea that media, religion, and culture are in an inseparable process of ongoing adaptation. While we think of them as separate concepts, it might enrich our thinking to have a single term for this process, perhaps *media/religion/culture*.

More typically people think of "media," "religion," and "culture" as quite distinct from each other, often talking about the impact of one upon the other.

But the more scholars study them in relationship to each other, the more we see that they are so integrated and interactive that we understand these concepts best when we think about them as an interactive system within which people establish and express their identities, and relate to that which they regard as sacred or transcendent, and through which they interpret the worlds they inhabit.

Today we see many examples of how religion is enmeshed with media in ways that make the two phenomena inseparable aspects of culture. To understand religion we have to understand media. Here are a few contemporary examples of how media and religion are integrated.

At a conference on Islam and media sponsored by the Center for Media, Religion, and Culture at the University of Colorado at Boulder (January, 2010) a young, urban Arab-American Muslim performs rap music to express an identity which is simultaneously Arab and American and to explore what it means to be Muslim in a context so different from that of his immigrant parents. He is a graduate student who also writes academic papers about this practice. For him, Muslim identity is something being constructed and articulated through the forms of popular music and academic writings. Both require a conversation between the inherited sacred writings and traditions and his contemporary location.

Trekkers, a 1997 documentary film about *Star Trek* fans, portrays a woman who seems to confuse her role as an officer in the fan club with being an actual officer on the starship *Enterprise*. When called to jury duty, she wears her *Star Trek* uniform. Asked why, she explains that *Star Trek* expresses the values of justice that should guide her service. For her, the fan club serves as a center of meaning-making ritual activity that seems very much like religious community. The *Star Trek* films and television episodes are the sacred texts that provide the moral lessons that guide her practice (see Figure 1.1).

Figure 1.1 Star Trek convention

The instructor of an online class at a Bible college leads students in a virtual communion service. Later a group of theologians, meeting online, debate whether this can be a legitimate Christian practice. For the class, the Internet has become a location for their religious life, and for the theologians it provides space to discuss both the boundaries of religious practice and the importance of the physical body in Christian practice (Duce 2013).

In each of these examples people use media, religion, and culture to understand, articulate, and embody identity. For them, media are not merely an external source of entertainment or information but a cultural expression they can draw on, appropriate, and remake to express religious and cultural identity. These vignettes illustrate that some people use media spaces to create religious selves, as space for religious practice, or as a public square within which they discuss religion.

Human beings inhabit media cultures, making it difficult to imagine other ways of engaging the world around us or to think clearly about how our own experiences of religion and media are connected. To draw on an old analogy, we are like fish asked to think about water. Because the fish is dependent on the omnipresence of water, it cannot imagine a world without water and thus cannot think about the significance of water in its life. Media are the water most of us swim in. Like the fish, many of us have trouble imagining a different world and thus recognizing the significance of the media environments within which we "swim."

Media, Religion and Culture draws on examples from many different religions and cultures. Some of these will be familiar to you; others will be new and may seem strange. In addition to reflecting on how other people integrate religion and media, you might want to think about how media and religion may be part of your own experience and identity. Many people today do not simply inherit their identity—including their religious identity—from their parents or community. In many societies they are free to choose between religions, or choose to practice no religion. Or, they create and express personal religious identities by drawing on many influences, including family and community traditions, and the media they consume and create.

Consider your own media location and religious identity. To what extent do you think of yourself as religious, spiritual, or secular, and how is that expressed in your life? Are you part of a religious group? Do you have personal spiritual practices? Were these practices passed down in your family, or have you adopted them on your own?

What entertainment and news media do you consume, and how do they inform the way you think about the world and about what it means to be human? Do you use social media such as Facebook, Twitter, or Second Life to present a portrait of yourself to the world? Consider the movies and television you watch, the video games you play, videos you may produce, and the social networks of which you are a part. What do your media practices suggest about the dreams, wishes, and commitments which make you uniquely you? What do they suggest about your understanding of the world you inhabit and the sources you draw from for meaning and direction?

It is tempting to think of the relationships between religion and media described here as a new phenomenon, perhaps emerging with the development of radio, cable television, or the World Wide Web. People ask, often with alarm, how these new media are changing religion. In doing so they often imply that religion was once a fixed and unchanging reality that is now beset by change. They worry that the pure essence of religion is diluted as it finds expression in new forms. This book suggests that this is not in fact a new phenomenon. Religion and media have always existed in relationship to each other, overlapping, serving some of the same functions, and changing in response to each other. In studying religion in any period or context we can and should ask how religion is mediated and ponder the implications of this mediation.

Key terms: culture, religion, and media

Having argued that we ought to think about media, religion, and culture in relationship to each other, this introductory chapter will none-the-less separate the terms. This makes it possible to look more closely at these key terms. After defining more clearly what is suggested by media, by religion, and by culture, the following chapters will return to thinking of them in their interactive totality.

Culture can be thought of as everything human beings make and maintain through language, ritual activity, and construction. It includes art, architecture, and technologies, but also the social structures that define power relationships: kinship, government, race, class, gender, and so forth. A culture is an ongoing project of group identity construction. The things we make and maintain create a portrait of us as a people. These cultural portraits establish boundaries; they tell us who is included and who is not. We misunderstand a culture if we fail to recognize its boundaries and the way its boundaries change over time. One can think of culture broadly, in terms of national and language cultures, but also on a smaller scale: pop, folk, and ethnic cultures, as well as media cultures that often transcend the boundaries between other cultural forms.

Media, religion, and culture are inseparably engaged in a process of ongoing adaptation. Religion shapes and is shaped by other elements in society. Changes in technology, in political organization, and in communications and media lead to cultural change, including changes in religion. And cultures adapt in response to new religious possibilities. There is give and take to this ongoing process.

Religion at first seems simple to describe and then quickly becomes complicated. There are many competing definitions to be found in the discussion of religion. People often begin with the assumptions of their own religion or those of the dominant religion in their society and then expand their definitions as they become aware of expressions of "religion" that do not quite fit their definition.

Many people see religion as a matter of belief, focusing on one or more central deities, such as the God of Judaism, Islam, or Christianity, or the gods in Hinduism or Greek mythology. But this definition seems inadequate when they start to consider types of spirituality that do not revolve around a central deity such as that of some Native Americans, Buddhists, or Taoists.

Another approach in defining religion is to describe it in terms of practice and ask what adherents of religion do with their bodies. You can see that they go to particular places that they regard as sacred, they carry out rituals at particular times, and they observe rules about how they should and should not behave.

Yet another approach suggests that religion is to be understood by the way it makes some things sacred and others profane. In this sense religion serves to set apart and protect what the practitioners understand to be sacred from the everyday messiness of life.

There are many ways to describe this complex area of human life. Here are two sample definitions from respected commentators on religion:

- Anthropologist Clifford Geertz (1973: 90) writes,

A religion is a system of symbols which acts to establish powerful, pervasive, and long-lasting moods and motivations in [people] by formulating conceptions of a general order of existence and clothing these conceptions with such an aura of factuality that the moods and motivations seem uniquely realistic.

- Religious studies scholar Robert A. Orsi (2004: 4) suggests that

religion is the practice of making the invisible visible, of concretizing the order of the universe, the nature of human life and its destiny, and the various dimensions and possibilities of human interiority itself, as these are understood in various cultures at different times, in order to render them visible and tangible, present to the senses in the circumstances of everyday life.

Notice that Geertz thinks of religion as a "system of symbols" that establish particular ways to act in society, while Orsi thinks of religion as a "practice" related to the interior life and how we understand the meaning of the universe. As you listen to other people describe religion and develop your own working definition, pay attention to which of the multiple dimensions of belief and practice are included and consider what that suggests about what is central to religion.

Those who study and try to describe religion typically do so in one of three ways. Some think of religions primarily in terms of the God or ultimate concern around which the religion is organized. Others proceed descriptively, teasing out the practices of those who identify with the religion. Still others think functionally, asking what purpose the religion serves for its practitioners and for society at large.

The first group believes that religion is best understood in terms of its relationship to a transcendent force that gives meaning to people's lives. Those who approach religion in this way call the participants "believers" and seek to define this transcendent something that they believe in. These students of religion try to understand the ideal form of human life that the believers are attempting to live out, and how this way of life is faithful to their under-standing of God, gods, or a sense of the transcendent to which they seek to be true. To see how this works, consider a particular religion with which many readers will be familiar: Christianity. Employing this first approach, one would tease out the distinctive claims that Christians make about God and Jesus, assuming that Christianity is best understood by clarifying what Christians believe and by contrasting that to what the adherents of other religions believe. Those who proceed in this way might also notice that the particularities of these claims are so important that Christians divide themselves into sub-groups based on their specific understandings of God and Jesus, and sometimes these groups further split and form new communities based on questions about doctrine and belief. Further, they might ask how Christians' distinctive beliefs inform their decisions in daily life.

The second approach describes religion by its rituals and distinctive practices, and thinks of those who participate in the religion as "practitioners." This approach suggests that religion is best understood and identified by looking at the actions of the people who practice it. Approaching religion in this way, those who study religion ask when and where the practitioners gather. What do they do with their bodies and voices? With respect to Christians they might observe that they tend to gather on a particular day for worship and that, though they have a variety of styles of worship, there seem to be some practices that most Christians hold in common such as forms of prayer, a holy meal, and so forth. In trying to understand the differences between various communities of Christians, scholars who think in this way would look at the differences in their practices rather than the differences in their beliefs. They might note that some are celibate and others marry or that some fold their hands to pray and others lift them skyward. For some the sermon seems the center point of worship and for others the holy meal, an altar call, or speaking in tongues. Extending this approach, researchers might look at the way Christian practitioners express their religious identity in their homes and communities, through actions such as praying at meals, displaying the Bible or pictures of Jesus or Christian saints in their homes, placing bumper stickers with Christian messages on their cars, or by carrying out acts of charity, social reform, or civic activism that they identify as forms of Christian witness.

The third approach defines religion by looking at its function in society. Such an approach thinks of religion as part of a larger society that is served by the religion. This approach looks less at the individual benefit of believing or practicing the religion and instead asks how society as a whole might benefit from it. Considering Christianity from this third perspective, some have sug-gested that the faith helps to provide order and stability to society by prescribing and proscribing certain behaviors and relationships. They observe that, starting with the Emperor Constantine in the third Century CE, governments have aligned themselves and their country with Christianity, and in so doing claimed the Christian God's blessing and asserted that their policies were expressions of the divine will. Some who think of religion in this way suggest that, when a religion's authority is invested in the existing social order, it inevitably justifies inequities in society, and point to the use of Christianity to justify the practices of slavery and gender inequality as distressing examples of this problem.

In a famous and influential book on the sociology of religion, first published in 1912, Emile Durkheim (2008) says that the function of religion is to distinguish areas of life that are set aside as sacred from others regarded as profane. Durkheim is particularly interested in what ties human communities together. He sees the function of religion as unifying a society by gathering a community around a shared understanding of what is sacred in order to establish a common morality. This leads him to assume that religion serves a conservative purpose, that it justifies existing social relationships in order to provide unity. Certainly we can think of examples in which religion serves that function. Others (Grimes 2002) argue that religious ritual can also serve a transformative function in society. These conflicting possibilities for how religion functions in society can be seen in the civil rights movement that began in the United States in the 1950s and '60s. As slaveholders had done in the defense of slavery, some people used religion to justify long-standing racial inequalities, resisting social change and suggesting that the existing social order expressed a divinely established hierarchy among the races. Others found resources in religious beliefs, texts, and practices that justified, required, and blessed a movement to change the social order. This was true among abolitionists who resisted slavery and later for Christians and Jews who found religious motivation to participate in the civil rights movement. In your own reflection, look for examples where religion serves a conserving function and for those where it serves a transforming function in society.

A further question is whether there is something irreducible about religion, something ineffable and unique that is distinct from media and culture. Some who have studied religion from the perspective of other disciplines suggest that religion is only an expression of other cultural forces and processes such as politics or economics. Noting that religion offers explanations of the natural world and the cosmos, some people suggest that religion is a proto-science replaceable by more replicable scientific processes. Others, seeing that religion can be a source of both conflict and unity in society, understand religion as a subset of law, government, or ethics. Those in religious and theological studies, however, usually argue that religion is "a distinctive space of human practice and belief which cannot be reduced to any other" (Asad 1993). Readers might ask, "Is there a conflict between the claim that religion is a unique sphere of practice and belief, and the assertion that media, religion, and culture are inseparable?" This question opens on to theological questions that are beyond the scope of this volume. The assertion here is simply that, while religion is a distinctive phenomenon, it cannot be seen apart from its location in culture, expressed through its changing mediations.

Although none of these approaches provides a full and adequate picture of religion, keep these various approaches to understanding religion in mind as you think about how religion and media interact and overlap. In describing religion strive for a definition broad enough to explain religion in both its institutional and emerging forms and to give a sense of what religion is like both for those who practice culturally dominant forms of religion and also for those at the margins of society who practice less known, minority forms of religious life.

Definitions help us draw clear distinctions between what is religion and what is not. However, the boundaries of religion are a much debated topic. Consider a few cases:

- As new forms of Buddhism emerge in the West, some who practice more traditional forms of the religion ask whether these new forms are recognizable as Buddhism.
- In describing the fervor of Elvis Presley's fans, particularly after his death, some people have used the religious concept of *veneration* to understand what the singer meant to his fans. They point to what they describe as "shrines" to the singer created by "followers" and describe their visits to his Graceland home as "pilgrimages" (Doss 1999). (See Figure 1.2.)
- One provocative study of religious movements in the US and South Africa (Chidester 2005) says that even "religious charlatans" can perform the work of religion. The author suggests that religious frauds and fakes can evoke a genuine religious response among their followers.

Does a reworked form of a religion still qualify as that religion? Can extreme adoration of a celebrity be likened to a religion? Can ostensibly fraudulent religious leaders end up doing religious work?

Figure 1.2 Elvis shrine

Attempting to define the boundary of what constitutes religion raises the question of whether everything that is described as religious belongs in the category. Some scholars (Ward 2011) question whether it adds to the clarity of our understanding to say that every aspect of media culture that scholars have described as religion is fully religion. Perhaps they are only similar to or like religion. This distinction suggests that culture provides material and practices that may not quite be religion, but that we could understand them better by considering how they are like religion.

For now, think of religion as a human activity of practice and belief through which we connect the everyday to something we hold to be ineffable, transcendent, or sacred. Religion includes theological ideas about what is sacred, but religion is more than ideas. It is embodied in ritual activities such as bathing, kneeling, lighting candles, pilgrimage, and forms of religiously motivated public service or social action. Further, religion by its sense of the sacred and its activities serves some function in society. For good or ill, it makes a difference.

The term *media* also needs to be defined. Though we often talk as though its meaning is self-evident, the definition of "media" may be as contested as that of "religion."

People often think of media as a modern phenomenon that began with technologies such as the telephone, radio, or the movies. But, as long as people have been communicating, there have been media. Speech is one early medium, cave painting another. From these earliest human efforts to communicate, to pass on their thoughts, concerns and experiences, people have been developing new ways to communicate. Typically, new forms of media serve an amplification process. They allow us to reach a wider audience. Think, for example, about how writing made it possible to preserve and pass on a message, and how printing made it possible to cheaply prepare many copies of a message, sharing the written message with far more people.

These forms of communication can be said to *mediate* an idea, practice, or experience. What do we mean by *mediate*? Regis Debray suggests that the common word "communication" leads us to misunderstand the process of sending a message. Messages do not simply travel unchanged from one person to another. Rather, Debray says that both "sender and receiver are modified from the inside by the message they exchange, and the message itself modified by its circulation." He uses *mediation* to refer to this complex process. Thinking about the means of this mediation, Debray cites Peter-Paul Verbeek, who says,

> Things play a role precisely in this relationship between human and world. ... Human beings act with the help of artifacts and perceive through them. This role of things can be characterized as *mediation*. Things ... mediate how human beings are present in their world and how the world is present to them.
>
> (Debray 1996: 44)

To understand these processes of mediation or communication requires attention to more than just the technical capacities of media and the way they change with the emergence of new media. Understanding them requires attention to what human beings do with media. Above, in defining religion, it was argued that we need to pay attention to religious *practice*: that religion cannot be understood as only a matter of belief and doctrine. Rather, we have to pay attention to what people do with those beliefs and doctrines, to the way they organize their lives in relationship to them. A similar claim could be made about media, that the concept is best understood by paying attention to people's media practice. How do media practices organize individual and community lives?

If mediation refers to both the complex process through which we, our hearers, and our messages are changed in the act of communication and the artifacts through which this process happens, what does it mean to mediate religion? Working from Orsi's definition of religion as the "process of making the invisible visible," cited above, we can see that mediating religion involves both the "things" (language, actions, smells, and sounds, as well as texts, images, and so forth) through which religion is expressed and the way that all of the actors involved (religion itself, as well as the senders and receivers) are changed by the process of communicating about religion.

Understood in this way media are not merely carriers of messages. They are perhaps lenses through which we engage the world around us, shaping—as much by their form as their content—our perceptions of what constitutes reality. This process cannot be understood by focusing only on the technologies of communication; it is found also in the uses that human beings make of technologies. We are not powerless in the face of the media sphere, but we must work within its possibilities and limitations. Having a presence in the media confirms our importance, even our existence, and absence or exclusion from the media fundamentally questions our relevance. As we will see more clearly later, religion is shaped by the media culture it inhabits. If Muslims are only represented in the media by images of fundamentalist terrorists, young Muslims trying to articulate an identity that is both Islamic and modern may feel invisible and unheard. The young Muslim rapper described earlier expresses his identity by pushing back and making an Islamic American space for himself, however small, in a larger media culture.

There are many different forms of media, and each medium communicates in quite different ways. This distinction between *media* and *medium* is not simply a concern about grammar. When people use media in the singular, as in the claim "The media promotes violence and sexism" or "The media provides a distorted picture of religion," they are making an ideological argument that the disparate forms of media speak with a single voice that articulates the values of the controlling elite. However, we might ask whether media is a singular block of power that besieges and transforms culture. Are Fox News, MTV, Twitter, and the website of a desert monastery really part of a monolithic force with a single message or effect on society? When people speak about media using a plural verb, saying, "Media *wield* great influence on our opinions" rather than "the media *wields* a great influence," or when they speak of the implications of a particular medium in a particular cultural context, saying for example, "Evangelical television serves to confirm the identity of an Evangelical audience rather than to convert non-believers," they recognize the complex relationship between audiences and various forms of media.

Religion as a dynamic process

One common misunderstanding about the interaction of religion and media is based in the assumption that religion is a fixed and unchanging reality that transcends the cultures within which it is embedded. This misunderstanding of religion, perhaps rooted in the fact that religion makes truth claims about ultimate reality, leads to the suggestion that media are a singular cultural force that impinges on religion, changing it in ways that dilute what is assumed to be religion's pure, transcultural, original form. When religion is viewed positively, this approach suggests that media developments cause religion to turn away from some idealized pre-mediated past. When religion is viewed negatively, the approach suggests that religion is passive and anachronistic, while media are progressive and dynamic. But if religion has always been mediated and if many different media are affecting and being affected by this changing religious process, then we are trying to describe a much more complicated human process.

Media cultures

It should be clear by now that the term *media* is not meant to signify a monolithic entity speaking with one voice to compel social conformity or change. Rather, there are different, identifiable periods and regions shaped by a medium of communication or the interaction of several media. The internal logic of this system of communication, interacting with other cultural factors, enables what we might call a *media culture.* That is a culture that is defined by the logic inherent in the dominant forms of mediation and by the ways of being in the world which they encourage. The Enlightenment, for instance, emerged in a period of growing literacy in Europe. Learning to read and write encourages a particularly linear system of logic. Letters add up to words that in turn add up to sentences and paragraphs gradually advancing an argument, idea, or narrative. Thus learning to read and write initiates one into a system of thinking based on the assumption that knowledge is built in this linear development fashion. The practice of reading aloud in groups encourages the sense of shared under-standings and community identity. In contrast, the practice of silent reading separates the reader from the family or community, encouraging a sense of the individual self and even more the individual interpreter.

If the media culture created by writing and literacy encouraged a linear way of knowing, how have later media developments produced contrasting ways of knowing? Marshall McLuhan famously said that "the medium *is* the message"

(1964). He suggests that television encourages a different kind of knowing, one less linear and more synthetic, where viewers are obliged to pay attention to everything in the image at once. Where the developments in philosophy, theology, politics, and literature of the Enlightenment were the products of the careful linear logic and careful distinctions taught by literacy, electronic media culture rests on gestalt thinking in which the viewer takes in multiple layers of content simultaneously and produces meaning in the interplay. With the emergence of digital media and the Internet, we are living through a period of media change as significant as the emergence of print and the spread of literacy. In a relatively short time computers, cell phones, and various technologies for audio and visual recording have emerged. The Internet and its cyberspaces have become ubiquitous, and new patterns of meaning making emerge based on their logics.

It can be tempting to give sole credit or blame to technology for this new culture. One of the critiques of McLuhan's thought is that it expresses a sort of technological determinism, as though new media make particular cultural changes inevitable. It is more accurate to recognize that new media open new ways of communicating and practices *and* that people respond to them in a variety of ways. Media cultures emerge not only out of media change, but out of the choices that people make about how to use, resist, or adapt new technologies. Clearly a new media culture is emerging influenced by the development of digital media, but it will be best understood by studying the choices people make about how to use these new digital tools and spaces.

Changing media spaces

In thinking about the World Wide Web, most people probably conclude that it is a source of information through which one can gather data and learn of events as near and personal as the breakup of a couple you know and as distant and public as political revolutions in distant lands. However, the emerging media culture of the Web cannot be understood only in terms of the flow of information. Like changes in media in the past, the transition to digital media culture involves more than a shift in communication technology. The Web provides a media space where people play games, have meetings, and create complex communities. On the Web, technologies merge and interact, and those who have access are instantly connected. To understand this networked media culture it is not enough to note that messages are sent and received more quickly. In the contemporary media culture, people use these technologies and devices to create and express personal and community identity. These changes interact with other cultural elements, and new ways of envisioning the self and society emerge.

This change is happening at a much more rapid rate than was typical of media change in the past. Perhaps a personal example of this transition is helpful. I grew up in a mid-sized American city in the 1950s and '60s. My home had one telephone hardwired to the wall in the kitchen, a black-and-white television that got three channels affiliated with the then dominant national networks, and a radio and record player contained in a large cabinet that dominated the living room. My family shared these devices and negotiated how or when to use them. How we used them was part of our shared family identity. In that media culture, where access to media was shared, most media programming was designed to appeal to the entire family. It was an assertion of independence from the family when—perhaps in the fifth or sixth grade—I got a transistor radio and could listen to rock and roll.

While there were some advances in media technology including the popularization of color TV, the media world of my childhood was fairly stable. When I left home for college I took the portable typewriter that my mother had used when she was a college student, and I would not purchase my first primitive computer until I was writing my doctoral dissertation in the 1980s.

Consider how rapidly media culture has changed since then! Today children and young adults live in a markedly different media culture. They assume that a rapid rate of media change is to be expected. The multiple televisions in their homes access hundreds of channels, of which they may actually watch dozens. Rather than serving one big audience, television has become a location for a series of niche markets with specialized programming for every family member. Not only has television changed in my lifetime, a wide range of new forms of media have emerged allowing new ways of relating to media. Individuals can download movies on their personal devices, text and tweet, gather in media-generated "flash mobs," and express themselves by sampling and reassembling media, creating their own videos, maintaining Facebook and MySpace pages, blogging, and posting files on YouTube.

The point of this story is neither to bemoan nor overly idealize the change. Hopefully readers will notice that the rate of media change has accelerated and seems to continue to accelerate. Further, this media culture does more than quickly exchange messages. Rather, it connects people in networks locally and globally, providing both ways in which people can withdraw from society and new forms of human community. In the end, social media is as much a space for identity construction as a tool for passing messages.

In the midst of this changing media culture, religion adapts and reframes itself. One influential thinker in the field of religion and media suggests that today religion and media occupy the same "conceptual and practical space" (Hoover 2003). Following in that tradition, this book seeks to understand media, religion, and culture as integrated processes.

Discussion questions

1 What are the implications of the author's claim that media, religion, and culture are hyperlinked, that they should be thought of as "An inseparable process of ongoing adaptation?"

2 What is a media culture? What are some examples of new media cultures from the past and how did religion and society adapt to them?

3 What was surprising or interesting about the definitions of religion suggested in the chapter? Which of them seemed most helpful or appealing to you and why?

4 How would you define religion?

5 In the reflections that follow both Lofton (Oprah) and Stolow (telegraph) reflect on religion outside its usual institutional locations. What do their essays suggest about religion and its function in society?

References

Asad, Talal (1993) *Genealogies of Religion: Discipline and Reasons of Power in Christianity and Islam*, Baltimore, MD: Johns Hopkins University Press.

Chidester, David (2005) *Authentic Fakes: Religion and American Popular Culture*, Berkeley: University of California Press.

Debray, Regis (1996) trans. Eric Rauth, *Media Manifestos*, New York: Verso.

Doss, Erica (1999) *Elvis Culture: Fans, Faith, and Image*, Lawrence: University Press of Kansas.

Duce, Janice L. (2013) *A Theological Inquiry Regarding the Practice of the Eucharist in Cyberspace*, PhD dissertation, University of Denver and the Iliff School of Theology.

Durkheim, Emile (2008) trans. Carol Cosman, *The Elementary Forms of the Religious Life*, Oxford: Oxford World's Classics (first published in French in 1912).

Geertz, Clifford (1973) *The Interpretation of Cultures*, New York: Basic Books.

Grimes, Ron L. (2002) "Ritual and Media" in Hoover, Stewart M. and Lynn Schofield Clark, eds. *Practicing Religion in the Age of the Media: Explorations in Media, Religion, and Culture*, New York: Columbia University Press.

Hoover, Stewart M. (2003) "Religion, Media and Identity: Theory and Method in Audience Research on Religion and Media" in Mitchell, Jolyon and Sophia Marriage, eds. *Mediating Religion: Conversations in Media, Religion and Culture*, London: T&T Clark.

McLuhan, Marshall (1964) *Understanding Media: The Extensions of Man*, New York: McGraw-Hill.

Orsi, Robert A. (2004) *Between Heaven and Earth*, Princeton, NJ: Princeton University Press.

Ward, Pete (2011) *Gods Behaving Badly: Media, Religion, and Celebrity Culture*, Waco, TX: Baylor University Press.

Reflection

Consuming Oprah's products, consuming Oprah's spirit

Kathryn Lofton

The charismatic genius of Oprah Winfrey is, first, her ability to make her particularity something universal and, second, her unabashed desire to make her universal the subject of a multimedia empire. Oprah encourages consumption as a means to change the experience of living for her viewers (Figure 1.3). The practice of buying feeds internal and external change for such women, dressing and surrounding them with a material beauty that should be reflected in their spiritual interior. Like a lot of religious movements, she believes her adherents will look differently and act differently than everyone else; they will literally wear their sanctification.

Figure 1.3 Oprah magazine

This practice of gift giving and gift wearing reverberates throughout her empire. "The O Bracelet," for example, was "hand beaded by women in Rwanda and Zambia." *O Magazine* continues:

> Let's just assume (A) you know that women in Africa face a pileup of hardships—serial rape, AIDS, illiteracy, hunger, poverty, genocide. (B) You care and would like to help, although *how on earth* is the daunting question. (C) If we changed the subject to jewelry—hey, catch that sudden glint of spirit, the lift of pleasure? Without doubt, tiny bits of shimmer and color release slaphappy chemicals in the brain. (Science will prove it; you watch.)

The purchase advocated by Winfrey achieves climactic global effect. Uncomfortable observers, be at peace (the narrative proceeds): we aren't girls who just want to have bauble fun. We are girls distracted by a scientific slaphappy that is a glint of spirit around which anyone could rally. The article hawks: "So may we twist your arm into slipping on one of these bracelets?"

Purchasing is an act of spiritual politics for Oprah's imagined audience. We learn that the designer of the O bracelet was Mary Fisher, "the well-heeled suburban mother from a prominent family who stunned the country by announcing at the 1992 Republican Convention that she was HIV-positive." Mary "hit life running," spending "a lot of time in Africa" working with AIDS victims who are "blown away to meet a white woman with the disease, much less one sitting on the ground next to them, talking frankly and trading crafts skills. In Rwanda they call her *Mirarukundo*—'full of love.'" Mary then connected with Fair Winds Trading, an organization "that develops markets for the arts of the world's poorest." The bracelets will be sold exclusively at Macy's department store. Oprah promises that the purchase will make you feel good, "that you'll feel even better knowing how it's improved the life of the woman who made it for you. Call it an ethical luxury. A conscientious indulgence. If nothing else, it's a really good buy."

This is a powerful example of how consumer and political life are fused through a spiritual understanding of the self. "The O Bracelet" translates the globalizing complex in multiple ways, simultaneously selling a universal brand (the "O") in its form and name, collaborating multiple agencies, and bracing any nervous critics against the assault of polarization with the narrative of triumphant women overcoming disappointing men, befriending other women to "hit life running" as leaders of a new globalized economy of female empowerment and missionary purpose. Every confusion is alleviated by purchase. The moral is assured as the advertisement-as-article concludes: "If nothing else, it's a really good buy." The making of the *good* buy (how it is done, and for whom) is central to any description of the making of the American secular, and the spiritual that enfolds it.

Reflection
Telegraphing as spirit

Jeremy Stolow

Nestled on the back page of a November 1861 edition of *Harper's Weekly* appeared an image celebrating the inauguration of the first transcontinental telegraph line. Even more profoundly than the postal system and print industries that preceded it, the electromagnetic telegraph invoked a coming age of free exchange and virtual tele-presence. This new vision of wired nations and unchained spirits is dramatically depicted by the image of an angel, moving as lithely as a tight-rope walker along the telegraph wire, her wings folded in wait for an even more effortless journey to come (Figure 1.4). By the time its cables had reached the Pacific Coast, the telegraph had already come to occupy a prime place in the American imaginary, providing (among many other things) a metonym for the "kinetic revolution" that was placing new priorities on motion, transformation, and progress in all facets of civil, cultural, economic, and political life in the Jacksonian era. Long before Google, Second Life, or the Web 2.0, telegraphy was implicated in the creation of phantasmic, electrically mediated communities of knowledge-seekers, conversation partners, and like-minded souls dispersed across the entire globe.

Figure 1.4 Illustration from *Harper's Weekly*

The choice to depict the bearer of telegraphy's utopian gifts in the form of an angel was not unique to *Harper's* magazine, nor is it particularly surprising. The figure of the angel has been linked at least since St. Augustine to the idea of instantaneous travel, and angelic speech has been described as a transference of pure, interior thoughts from one party to another without any degradation or loss. "Angels," John Durham Peters (2012) summarizes, "are exempt from the supposed limitations of embodiment, and effortlessly couple the psychical and the physical, the signified and the signifier, the divine and the human. They are pure bodies of meaning."

But, as it so happens, angels were not the only spirit entities drawn to the telegraph line. An appreciation of telegraphy's transcendent, magical nature had already been well established in American popular culture. Not least in the case of Spiritualism, a movement whose development precisely overlapped with the rise of the telegraph. One particularly prescient observer of the telegraph's apparent promise to render distance obsolete was the Universalist minister and trance speaker, John Murray Spear. In 1854, Spear was the recipient of detailed plans, provided to him in a trance state by the spirit of Benjamin Franklin, for the construction of a "soul-blending telegraph." The soul-blending telegraph was an intercontinental telepathic transmission system to be powered by a corps of sensitized mediums installed in male/female pairs in high towers. This network of harmonized spirit mediums promised stiff competition with existing telegraph services, which were still beset by operational difficulties, and which had yet to announce success in the ongoing effort to connect distant continents. Spear thus imagined an imminent future of communicative harmony on a global scale, a utopian dream to which the crude workings of the electromagnetic telegraph only imperfectly pointed. Commenting on the (at the time, yet-to-be realized) project of the American industrialist, Cyrus Field, to lay a submarine telegraph cable across the Atlantic Ocean, Spear writes:

> The purpose is a laudable one, and should be encouraged; but it is seen that such a means of communication would be exceedingly expensive, and, of necessity, would rarely accommodate the poorer classes, while it would enrich others. It is a hazardous scheme—the most so of any proposed. *In that submarine wire lies the snake of a most dangerous monopoly.*

Who living in our contemporary moment, marked on the one hand by fantasies of hyper-connectivity and techno-transcendence, and on the other by the specter of sinister corporate intentions and digital divides, cannot hear the echo of Spear's cry?

Reference

Peters, John Durham (2012) *Speaking into the Air: A History of the Idea of Communication*, Chicago: University of Chicago Press.

2 Making and articulating religious identity

Key ideas

- Religion takes many forms in the media age, some communal and some more individual.
- In contemporary Western societies, secularization makes religion more private.
- The religious task, where religion is excluded from the public square, is often one of identity construction.
- People may hyphenate several religious traditions or sample from many in the process of their construction of a personal religious identity.

Traditions, communities, and institutions

Chapter 1 considered a variety of ways that people think about religion. For some, religion is a matter of ideas or beliefs about God, gods, or the sacred. For others it is a matter of practice. Historically, religion was something that people did together; they grouped themselves in communities organized by shared beliefs and practices. Even the hermit was part of a larger religious community that gave his or her solitude meaning. People found their identity in broad traditions such as Hinduism, Islam, Judaism, Buddhism, Christianity, and shamanism. Co-religionists shared a worldview rooted in common mythology, values, and ethos, and in shared activities. This shared religious practice was a powerful source of social unity, though it also produced conflict among and sometimes within communities.

Institutionalized forms of religion emerged around particular traditions of belief and practice. These institutions range from small local communities such as a mosque, temple, or church, to regional and transnational institutions like the Vatican. They have structures of authority, may own property, and often hold moral, economic, and political influence within the larger society. Now, in the digital age, they may exist wholly or partly online.

No religious institution fully encapsulates its larger tradition; there is no single example that fully embodies the possibilities of any large and long-established religion. For instance, those who self-identify as a Buddhist will likely affiliate with a particular Buddhist tradition, perhaps practicing *Theravada* or *Mahayana* Buddhism, and following cultural expressions within these movements. Their practice and beliefs might be shaped by Tibetan, Korean, or Japanese cultural expressions of Buddhism or by Western adaptations of these traditions. In these varied Buddhist contexts they develop beliefs about matters such as reincarnation and who has the authority to teach or perform rituals in their Buddhist community. They may develop particular local disciplines and practices.

The varied institutional expressions of a broader religious tradition may reflect language and cultural differences, or divisions over beliefs and practices, and systems of authority, conflicts over power and property, or other matters. Consider, for instance, how over time Christians divided themselves between Orthodox, Catholic, and Protestant expressions and then subdivided further into national churches, religious orders, and denominations.

To take but one example from the history of Christianity, John Wesley (1703–91) sparked a reform movement within the Church of England that led to the Methodist movement in the mid-eighteenth century and later to the establishment of separate Methodist churches. Continued reform movements established new institutional forms of the Methodist or Wesleyan branch of Christianity. In 1787, for instance, black Methodists in Philadelphia, chafing under racism and racial separation in the church, broke with the denomination to found the African Methodist Episcopal Church. Another split established the Free Methodist Church in 1860 partly in protest against the then common practice of charging worshipers for space in the pews. In the United States, immigrant European Methodists organized themselves into separate churches as well, creating places for worship that continued the language and practices of home. Methodist groups have split and recombined in new configurations, growing to become what is now the second largest Protestant group in the country and an institution with churches on six continents. Today Methodists continue to struggle over what unites and divides them, and some suggest that the largest Wesleyan body, the United Methodist Church, will split over whether gay people have a full place in the church. The process of growth and change in the Methodist Church has been duplicated in other Christian bodies. Thus, it may be more accurate to talk about "Christianities" rather than Christianity as a single integrated form of belief and practice. Similar patterns of unity and distinction exist in other religious traditions.

Where is religion located today?

In the mid-twentieth century, sociologists reflecting on the decline of organized religion in the West developed the idea of secularization (Berger 1967). They noted that, in complex modern societies, religion was becoming increasingly privatized, and secular institutions and the state itself were largely taking on the social and charitable functions once carried out by religious institutions. The sociologists concluded that religion was gradually going to fade away. Many of these thinkers forecasted, in fact, that in industrialized societies religion would have disappeared by now. Many religious institutions have lost members and influence. This is particularly true in the industrialized West, especially northern Europe, where religious identity and practice has markedly declined. In the global South, meanwhile, especially Africa and Latin America, both Pentecostal Christianity and Islam have spread. Even in the northern hemisphere religion has not died away; it continues to vie for space in the public square.

Certainly many people in modern societies, and in some places the majority, no longer identify themselves as religious. When secularity is the dominant form of public life, traditional forms of religion may be pushed to the margins. Religions continue to exist, but they involve fewer people, are more private than public, and have less influence on society. The secularization argument suggests that in such cultures religion has lost its power to provide unity and that other forms of social identity, ritual, and ethical discourse emerge to provide social coherence. This is an important phenomenon to recognize and raises the question of whether religion is simply one of many ways to explain and organize life.

In contrast to this perspective, another view is that religion fulfills certain essential purposes in society. According to this argument, in seemingly secular societies, religion has not disappeared; it has just taken new forms. In places where institutional forms of religion have lost influence, there has actually been a displacement of the core purposes of religion. People practice other types of ritual behavior that serve the functions of religion rather than activities that are classically "religious." There are many expressions of this displacement of religion away from traditional centers of religious life. One expression can be seen among people who describe themselves as spiritual without being religious; that is, they hold certain beliefs or have particular practices such as prayer, meditation, or the celebration of particular religious holidays without affiliating themselves with organized religion. Another expression of displaced religion can be found in civil religion. By invoking God in political speeches and on public monuments, articulating myths of national origin, or participating in rituals that venerate past leaders or the military dead, the nation itself becomes a location of the sacred. It is also argued that, when we idolize celebrities (Ward 2011) or participate in rituals of sports fandom (Evans and Herzog 2002), we are involved in practices that take on the forms and functions of religion. And some, such as Wiccans and other Neopagans, seek to return to forms of religion that have fallen out of favor with others.

Attention to what is happening "on the ground" suggests that there is continuous significant, if shifting, religious practice. While once-dominant forms of religion have become less common and lost influence, other forms of religion emerge or become more predominant. In some places, religions contest with each other for authority as one religion expands in influence and another shrinks. For example, the Buddhist and Hindu traditions are found in Europe and America partly due to migration but also due to conversion and the development of culturally distinct forms of practice. Similarly, Islam is increasingly part of the European and American religious environment.

Religion also takes other, less established forms. Some of these seem episodic and happen without clear structures and with informal transient leadership. In the United States, for instance, new forms of public mourning have emerged. Famous examples include the gatherings in New York's Central Park following the murder of former Beatle John Lennon and in a park near Colorado's Columbine High School after the infamous shootings took place there (Figure 2.1). In the aftermath of both public and private tragedies, informal and temporary "shrines" are established. People may gather in a public space at or near the location for ritual activities like singing, lighting candles, and giving memorial speeches. Prayers may or may not be offered. People often build "altars" on which they place pictures of the dead, poems, notes, and flowers. The music, speeches, and objects they leave may or may not include traditional religious references and symbols. Teddy bears, for example, have become a common talisman at sites where a child died.

Practices such as these also happen in virtual space as people use social media like Facebook or PostSecret as locations for confession and mourning. In a famous example of such a phenomenon, the sheer volume of response to pop star Michael Jackson's death was so large that it overwhelmed and shut down some forms of social media. These new forms of icon and ritual do not require the participation of official religious leaders, nor are they part of any ongoing institution or movement. Do they constitute "religion"? If so, do they suggest that religion is becoming less organized, more an effervescent experience that bubbles up in times of stress?

Figure 2.1 Site of Columbine High School shooting

New religious movements have arisen, such as the various forms of Neopaganism. Sarah Pike, who studies a variety of new religious movements, argues that we best understand what religion is doing by examining how it is practiced at the margins of society (Pike 2008). Some of these religious movements have emerged from within established religions, while others develop outside established patterns of religion. They may prove to be transitory, like the "cargo cults" which peaked in the 1950s in Polynesia, or become increasingly established, like the Church of Jesus Christ of Latter-day Saints or Scientology.

New media provide space for both conversation about religion and a location for religious experience. Websites like Patheos or Beliefnet contain blogs, essays, and question-and-answer forums about religion. These sites are independent and exist entirely online, there are others that are extensions of established face-to-face religious communities. As people feel freer to leave the traditions they were raised in, new religious movements emerge both off- and online, some as fleeting as the flowers and crosses at the site of a tragic accident.

Religion has not in fact disappeared. New forms of ritualization and meaning making steadily arise. In addition, traditional settings like the synagogue, ashram, church, mosque, or temple, and the traditions of which they are a part, remain powerful locations of religion in many places.

Constructing religious identities; media, hyphenation and sampling, and authority

In the preceding section we saw that religions contend for influence with one another and with secularity. In this process religion can provide social cohesion or serve as the location of conflict and difference. Change is not simply a modern phenomenon but an element of religion itself.

Stewart Hoover (2006) argues that in what he calls the current "media age" we see a distinctive change in how people understand and embody religion. Hoover argues that today the task of religion is one of constructing and articulating an individual religious self. This seems particularly to be the case in the West. Whether located within institutionalized religious communities, in loose networks, or entirely on their own, people are less likely to think of religious identity as something inherited from their forbears or expressed by a relationship to a single religious tradition. Whereas in the past religion was more clearly a matter of group identity, according to Hoover religious identities today often integrate ideas and practices from multiple sources. Rather than pursuing a particular tradition, individuals feel free to pick and choose from a range of available beliefs, practices, and symbols. New Age practitioners have been seen as a prime example of this individualized approach to religion. They draw on both Western and Eastern religions, often in conjunction with Jungian understandings of mythology and motivational psychology. But New Age religion is not characterized by any particularly doctrinal integration of these sources; rather individuals combine them in ways that are individually satisfying. One can find this same integrative practice among people who identify themselves within or between several traditional religious communities. There are, for example, individuals who simultaneously practice Christianity and Buddhism or Christianity and Islam (Frykholm 2011).

While it is taking place far more frequently today, the process of religious construction is not entirely new. Africans who were enslaved and brought to the Americas, for instance, came practicing Islam or the traditional religions of Africa. A part of their oppression was religious; they were forced to relinquish their own religions while Christianity was imposed on them. While many slaves and their descendants adopted Christianity, others resisted this imposition. Still others integrated their traditional practices with Christianity. One rich example of this can be seen in the practice of Candomblé, a religion that began among slaves in Brazil. Practitioners connected the Yoruba orishas (spirits or deities) with Catholic saints and developed unique expressions that continue to be practiced in Brazil and beyond (Capone 2010). Once while in Brazil I asked an Afro-Brazilian Catholic priest about Candomblé's integration of seemingly discordant religious elements. The priest replied, "Some say to us that you must choose between Candomblé and the Church, but we say," sweeping his arms widely open, "this is our religion." (See Figure 2.2.)

The influences of media

If this pattern of religious identity construction precedes the "media age," what does it have to do with media? Mass media have expanded our information about religious ideas and practices that differ from those of the communities within which we were raised. Social media provide settings for conversation about religion but also locations for practices and construction. So, the new

Figure 2.2 Candomblé practitioners with a statue of the orisha Iemanjá

media tools and locations that established religious communities and institutions increasingly used to connect their members, or invite others to join with them, make information and images about the gamut of religions more generally available. Media have become more complex than in the past, providing access to a wider range of voices. New forms of media such as the Internet give us access to a vast array of voices. Today, virtually anyone can have his or her own blog or website. This expansion of sources legitimates a wider range of religious authorities and makes it easier for people to "shop" for alternative voices.

New media do more than simply provide access to a wider range of information about religion. Instead, media model and encourage a constructionist way of building knowledge and articulating identity. Religious identity becomes something that one assembles from multiple sources, rather in the way that a hip hop artist creatively samples and repositions a musical phrase into an emerging composition. The way a wiki is constructed further illustrates this modern process of meaning-making. Wiki texts are not fixed; they undergo ongoing construction by multiple authors, who edit, sample, comment, and expand on them until it is impossible to point to a single author or unchanging text.

Personal identity is constructed in a similar way. Categories once assumed to be fixed, such as race, gender, and religion, seem fluid. More and more people do not allow their race to be defined by the box on a census form. Instead, they define themselves as biracial or multiracial. Gender, for many people, is not reducible to biology; it is a matter of performance, experienced and expressed in a variety of ways (Butler 1990). In similar ways, religion is not simply a matter of inheritance. Religion is constructed and performed, often with elements sampled from different traditions, even when, as with Candomblé, those traditions reflect religious worldviews that seem to be at odds with one another.

For many people, then, identity is an individual project. It is not inherited but chosen, developed, and performed. It might involve construction from multiple sources. Consider, say, a Presbyterian Protestant who attends retreats at a Roman Catholic monastery, a Jew-Bu (a cultural or religious Jew who also practices Buddhism), or someone who practices a complex form of New Age identification. Worshiping communities include many people who participate yet resist becoming members. The people who resist joining, it seems, are reluctant to let the tradition define their religious identity. Something similar is at play in those who identify as Catholic but reject particular church teachings such as those concerning birth control. The complex identities of these individuals exist at the meeting place of several religious communities or traditions.

American religion writer Cathleen Falsani (for links, see cathleenfalsani.com) exemplifies the way religious identity is created and performed in relationship to media. Her writing is far more personal than is typical of religion journalism; the traditional membrane between the personal and the public is quite porous in her work, and her own complicated religious identity becomes part of the story. She identifies as an Evangelical, yet some years ago she became a "Dudist" priest by sending money to a quasi-religious group that has grown up around the Coen Brothers' film *The Big Lebowski*. Dudists celebrate the film's witty combination of California slacker culture and the pop-Buddhism of its protagonist, "The Dude." Their proclamation of a *Dudist religion* is usually understood as an ironic comment on religion and their extreme interest in the film. Over the years Falsani came to call herself, with an interreligious chuckle, the "Dude-i-vata." It is tempting to think of this as mere language play about religion, a joke not to be confused with her "real" Christian life. But, she reported performing a wedding in July of 2010 using her Dudist credential. Presumably for the couple and community that gathered, this was not an ironic parody of religious ritual. Surely, then, Falsani's identification as the Dude-i-vata must be understood in some way as a part of her religious life.

Hyphenation and sampling

There seem to be two distinct tendencies or paths that people follow in the individual projects of religious identity construction described in this chapter. The social processes that are at play here could be termed *hyphenation* and *sampling*. These are concepts that are related but different.

The term *hyphenation* points to the linking of distinct traditions by a common factor, an occurrence that is often signified linguistically with a hyphen. With respect to religion, hyphenation is taking place when an individual simultaneously embraces two or more traditions in such a way that his or her participation in one cannot be understood without acknowledging the other. Thus, someone who is simultaneously participating in Hinduism and Christianity could be thought of as a "Hindu-Christian" or a "Christian-Hindu." This phenomenon is similar to what is signaled when one or both partners in a relationship choose to hyphenate their last names. Recognizing that they are part of two families of origin, the partners do not choose one name over the other or move back and forth between them. Instead, they point to both names and families as being part of their identity. The couple itself, then, serves as a point of integration between separate entities.

Sampling, introduced above, is a practice regularly employed by recording artists and hip hop DJs. Sampling refers to the way musicians borrow a musical phrase from another work and embed it in a new esthetic context, often giving it new meaning by the way they juxtapose it with other musical elements. In the broader digital culture, visual images and texts are used in a similar way. Artists gather materials from disparate sources, combining them into something that is new and unique. Applied to religion, sampling denotes how people appropriate images, objects, practices, and beliefs from religious traditions and use them in new ways without necessarily identifying themselves as part of the tradition from which they sample. Think of a woman who displays a statue of the Buddha in her home, intending it as a spiritual expression but without further embracing Buddhist practices. Perhaps she also listens to Gregorian chants to aid with meditation but does not identify herself as a Christian, or she has memorized passages from the *Tao Te Ching* but does not consider herself Taoist. Perhaps she unites a sense of karma and rebirth with pre-Christian

Celtic images and Native American practices. The woman is *sampling* these sources. Her relationship with the sources is more fragmentary than in cases of hyphenated religious identity. Religious practitioners, such as this woman, who sample, function as consumers who construct a religious self out of material from multiple sources. For them, validity lies in this rich self that they construct.

Some critics see approaches to religion such as hyphenation and sampling as "smorgasbord religion," where people adopt what they like about a religion and leave on the table what they do not. However you judge these approaches, hyphenation and sampling seem to be a part of the way religion continues to adapt and change in our day. Observers of religion need to see these practices accurately, understand what they mean to the participants, and ask how they influence the broader culture in which they happen.

What are the consequences of these contemporary forms of religious belief and practice? As will be argued more fully in Chapter 3, the emergence of new media with their multiple voices and interactivity has decentered traditional centers of authority and provides a model for the trend toward a religious identity crafted from multiple religious sources. Media culture accelerates the modern focus on individual identity and conscience. It invites the individual to construct a religious identity out of bits of loosely integrated beliefs and practices gathered from multiple sources.

Religious authority

When people claim the personal authority to shape their individual religious identity, traditional forms of religious authority are challenged. What does religious authority look like in contemporary media cultures? It is hard to remember that even so basic a source of authority as sacred writings emerged in a particular period and have been interpreted and venerated in different ways. It could be argued that leaders, tradition, and writings have less authority than they once did, or that they are granted authority in new and different ways by practitioners in the contemporary media age. Fundamentalism within various religions can be understood in part as resistance to this relaxing of traditional forms of religious authority.

What do these reflections tell us about the nature of religion and the relationship between religion and media as they are lived out today? Religion is fluid. People increasingly think of religion as an individual practice and are consequently constructing religious identities from multiple sources. In the current media culture traditional religious institutions and movements will certainly lose authority, as we see in the loosening of denominational commitment among many transient Christians in North America. When they move from one part of the country to another, Americans are likely to seek the religious community that "meets their needs" rather than attend the closest church of the denomination they grew up in.

It is not that people do not consult traditional sources of religious authority but that they often do so with a consumer's mentality. Rather than seeking to conform to patterns of religion preserved in sacred texts, handed down by tradition, or articulated by clergy and teachers, they are inclined to ask what is useful to them or what confirms and supplements their existing assumptions. How does this picking and choosing affect the traditions? How does it affect the practitioners? Religion serves multiple functions. It appears that the practice of constructing religion from disparate sources provides the confirmation of individual identity and values that religion in its traditional form often provides. But does a customized religion have the content and authority to challenge the practitioner's individual and societal assumptions and social behaviors, another traditional function of religion?

In summary, in digital culture people seek out religion and/or adopt practices and beliefs from multiple traditions that meet their individual needs. Modern media give them greater access to a broad range of religious practices and beliefs. This construction of the individual religious self reflects a shifting of authority. From the multiple voices that are present the individual can, and perhaps must, choose. A particular teacher or tradition, or some portion of the teaching or tradition, has authority because the individual grants it, usually in conjunction with other competing sources of authority.

Discussion questions

1 The author suggests that it is more accurate to talk about "Christianities" than Christianity. What does this distinction add to our understanding of this particular religion and to the phenomenon that is *media, religion, and culture*? Do you find this a helpful distinction? Why or why not?

2 What is secularization? Where do we see evidence of secularization? How have media been part of the process of secularization? How does religion change when the secular expands?

3 Discuss the physical sites of public mourning that have been established to commemorate tragic deaths. What objects, messages, and practices are typically included in these sites? Who is "in charge" of such sites? Are these sites religious? How, or how not? What does the existence of sites suggest about the role of organized religion today?

4 Discuss the idea that people construct a *religious self*, and the ways that contemporary media culture contributes to the expectation that identity construction is a central task of religion. Identify examples of such identity construction, either from the chapter or from your own observation. How is this similar to, or different from, how religion has been practiced in the past?

5 How are understandings of religious authority changing? What new models of authority does the chapter suggest are emerging? Do you see evidence of this?

6 The reflections that follow present two quite different images of contemporary media. Schofield Clark examines how a young Ethiopian immigrant uses digital media to express his identity, while Ward considers how mainstream media turn celebrities into demi-gods. What do these examples suggest about the power of media and about the way people shape or are shaped by contemporary media?

References

Berger, Peter L. (1967) *The Sacred Canopy: Elements of a Sociological Theory of Religion*, New York: Anchor Books.

Butler, Judith (1990) *Gender Trouble*, New York: Routledge.

Capone, Stefania (2010) *Searching for Africa in Brazil. Power and Tradition in Candomblé*, Durham, NC: Duke University Press.

Evans, Christopher H., and William R. Herzog, II (2002) *The Faith of Fifty Million: Baseball, Religion and American Culture*, Louisville, KY: Westminster John Knox Press.

Frykholm, Amy (2011) "Double Belonging: One Person, Two Faiths," *The Christian Century*, January 14.

Hoover, Stewart M. (2006) *Religion in the Media Age*, New York: Routledge.

Pike, Sarah M. (2008) "Religion," in Morgan, David, ed., *Key Words in Religion, Media and Culture*, New York: Routledge.

Ward, Pete (2011) *Gods Behaving Badly: Media, Religion, and Celebrity Culture*, Waco, TX: Baylor University Press.

Reflection
When Gods fall (off their bike)

Pete Ward

Early in 2013 an interview with Oprah Winfrey made headlines across the world. The cyclist Lance Armstrong, seven times winner of the *Tour de France*, confessed to being a drugs cheat. There had been rumors over a number of years, but when the news broke disbelief quickly turned to anger. Four months after the interview one young fan from Syracuse expressed the feeling of many, "It's just sad and it's just an awful thing because he was like my idol, but now I lost all respect for him."[1] Speaking on CNN, Betsy Andreu, the wife of a cyclist and former team mate of Armstrong, expressed frustration at the confession.

> I was willing to give him a chance and that's how he responds? Lance can redeem himself but only if he comes clean to the USADA and WADA because there is no way he conducted the biggest fraud in sports history on his own.[2]

Journalists spoke of the demise of a figure who had been worshiped by fans. Ali Khaled said that Armstrong, just like so many other sports stars, has proven himself to be the latest "idol with feet of clay."[3] CNN said that Armstrong's confession to Winfrey represented a "fall from grace."[4] (see Figure 2.3.)

Figure 2.3 Oprah Winfrey interviews Lance Armstrong

Lance Armstrong is hardly unique in his disgrace. He joins a long list of fallen sporting figures from OJ Simpson to Tiger Woods and Oscar Pistorius. Though commonplace, the demise of a sports star is always greeted with disbelief. Some kind of bond between the star and the wider public has been broken. In coming to terms with this rupture, the language of religion has taken centre stage. The media likes to talk of them as "fallen idols." This implies that they were figures who were once worthy of worship but no longer; but on closer inspection the word "idol" casts some doubt. Idols are not real Gods; they are false, and this is a clue to unpacking the religious and non-religious dynamics in celebrity worship.

Lance Armstrong's significance goes way beyond his sporting prowess. Let's be honest, no one but the French are really bothered about cycling. It is hardly the NFL or world cup soccer for that matter. That is not to belittle the massive achievement of winning the Tour seven times, something no one has ever done before. The real story about Armstrong is that he did this after he had been diagnosed with multiple forms of cancer, fought the disease, and broke through to recovery. It was his struggle with the big "C" that jettisoned him into public consciousness. He was someone to be admired, to be respected, to look up to, and to be inspired by. Anyone who had been touched by illness and adversity could identify with him and find something in his story to help them on their own journey. This in essence was the "connection" between Armstrong and the public. This connection was powerful and significant, but it was never religion. No one really worshiped him, there was no Church of Lance, no Armstrong shrine to visit. Lance was always an idol. The sacred doesn't reside in the sports star: it is located in the fan. The journey of the self is what is of the deepest religious significance. The religious metaphors of the journalist are attached to figures such as Armstrong, but their real point of reference is the ongoing struggle of the individual towards making the most of themselves and not letting themselves go. This is the true religious discipline and the real cult of the celebrity.

Notes

1 http://centralny.ynn.com/content/top_stories/631225/fans-react-to-lance-armstrong-s-admission, accessed May 1, 2013.

2 www.dailymail.co.uk/sport/othersports/article-2264338/Lance-Armstrong-confession-Oprah-Winfrey-How-world-reacted.html#ixzz2LRU7GM2e, accessed May 1, 2013.

3 www.thenational.ae/thenationalconversation/sport-comment/a-very-dark-period-for-sport#ixzz2LRXNko00.

4 http://edition.cnn.com/2012/10/22/sport/lance-armstrong-profile-cycling-usada, accessed May 1, 2013.

Reflection

Digital storytelling and narratives of identity
Abel's story

Lynn Schofield Clark

"Mkerew mkerew enbi kale mekera ymkerew." This is an Ethiopian proverb that Abel's grandmother taught him. It means, "Advise him and advise him. If he refuses to listen, let trouble advise him." When Abel produced a digital story as part of an after-school project, he chose to begin with this proverb. "That still motivates me to keep on pushing forward," Abel says in his story. "And now, I listen the first time so that I don't have to let the consequences teach me."

Abel's grandmother meant a great deal to him. She raised him as an Orthodox Christian in Ethiopia for nearly 12 years. Then, she helped him to move to the United States to live with his father so that he would have a better education and more opportunities.

During the summer after Abel graduated from high school, Abel's grandmother became gravely ill. His father traveled to Ethiopia to be with her, leaving Abel to care for himself for several weeks. And then, Abel suffered a number of discouraging setbacks. He began to wonder whether or not he would achieve his dream of attending college and, out of his despondency, he started making some bad decisions.

Abel had presented his digital story as if he were a finished product: "Now, I listen the first time so that I don't have to let the consequences teach me," he'd said. Yet, only a few months later, he found that consequences of his actions were once again teaching him. Once again, he found himself shaking his head, realizing that it was indeed better to listen for the wisdom of those who loved him than to wait for trouble to teach him. And once again, he had to seek and find forgiveness. Perhaps the hardest part was forgiving himself for not being quite as finished with the lesson as he had thought he was.

Abel also had to apologize to one of his friends, and that was hard. But that friend told him, "Look back at that story you made, and remember what your grandmother said. Use that story to remind yourself of how much she loved you and wanted the best for you." Abel's other friends agreed. In that moment, the digital story became more than a school project. It became an anchoring narrative, a narrative of aspiration that helped Abel to remember who he was and who those who cared about him wanted him to be.

This is the strength of the digital storytelling format in relation to self-development and, by extension, faith formation. He could refer to it in difficult times to recall those who had seen it and who knew him, both in his struggles and in his triumphs. The digital story became more than an end-product or a media production. It became a source of well-being, connected to other sources of well-being that included friends, family members, and his broader ethnic and faith communities.

Figure 2.4 Abel

It can be frustrating to realize that we do not live perfectly, that we do not progress to greater and greater virtue. It's a painful lesson, but it's a lesson of humanity. When a digital story can provide us with anchoring narratives that help us to remember who we are and who those we love most want us to be, they can serve as important bridges to our faith journey. They can remind us to pause, breathe, and listen. In this way, these mediated moments can help us to remember not to surrender to our worst, but that we are called by our faith and our community into our best (Figure 2.4).

3 Believing and practicing in a digital world

Key ideas

- New media provide spaces where religion is practiced.
- Religion is expressed in the way that practitioners consume, comment on, and commemorate both religious and seemingly secular experiences.
- Participation in media worlds is not necessarily passive; people often critically and creatively engage with the media that they consume.
- Participating in media culture can itself take on some of the form and function of religion.

New media are not simply fresh tools of communication, amplifying voices in new ways. Rather, new forms of media make possible new ways of thinking, new practices and rituals, and new ways of relating. To understand the digital culture that is emerging, students of media, religion, and culture look for places where new media, with their capacities for sampling and hybridity, become part of religious practice and ask what religion looks like in these new media spaces.

Religious change is not a new phenomenon. There are many examples of how religions have changed as people try out new ideas and practices in new cultural and media contexts. Consider the development of the Sunni and Shi'a traditions as distinct ways of being Muslim, or the way that the American "Beat" poets of the 1940s and '50s adopted and adapted Zen Buddhism to their context and purposes, or the way access to radio gave birth to new Evangelical voices.

Our current digital society is not the first to experience religious change, but still it is important to think how religion is changing in the digital culture. The pace of change seems quicker than it did in the past. Understandings of authority seem to be changing. Even among those who continue traditional forms of religion, fewer people submit to the authority of the tradition. Instead, they regard themselves as holding the authority to decide what they accept and reject from the tradition and how they practice. There seems to be an eclectic spirit at work today. Rather than seeing religious traditions as requiring forced choices, people feel free to "sample" and combine elements into their more individualized religious identities.

This chapter explores some of the implications of the way people work with inherited and adopted material to construct religious identities. They use media to express identity and establish community. When people tweet, *"Insha'Allah"* (God willing) or respond to a Facebook post saying, "Thanks be to God," they bring their religious life into the social media space and find religious community there. People also use these media spaces to comment on religion, or on social issues from a religious perspective. Popular speaker and public intellectual Diana Butler Bass has over 4,500 "friends" on Facebook where she often provides a liberal Protestant perspective on religious matters. Often her provocative posts receive dozens of comments and reposts. Brick-and-mortar temples, synagogues, and churches often have elaborate online sites, while other religious spaces seem to exist only or primarily online. For example, at Prarthana.com you will find a site providing "online Hindu Temple services." Should you want to travel to pilgrimage sites in India to offer *puja* (a form of worship in which an object, or the mind, body, or soul are offered to God), you can make arrangements through the website. But it is also possible to perform "online *puja*." The site is not only a source of information or support for embodied worship elsewhere but a location for religious practice.

Consumption: active and passive, reading and performing, and prosumption

One lively conversation about religion, particularly in capitalist cultures, draws on a wider examination of how people use consumption to express religious identity. Some suggest that people participate in religion by purchasing religious goods such as devotional art, prayer beads, books, and so forth. This seems, at least at first, a more passive form of religious life than the constructive practice and belief we have considered to this point. Consumption has been said to encourage this passivity, allowing powerful market forces to shape people's values and attitudes.

The argument that religion can be consumed starts with the observation that the objects and images we surround ourselves with say something about us. Sometimes this connection between object or image and identity is direct and straightforward. When the great Brazilian soccer player Pelé wore his uniform, it signified that he was a soccer player and a part of a particular team. When he played for Brazil in the World Cup, the uniform symbolized something larger and more complex about his identity. Not only did it show that Pelé was Brazilian, the uniform was a symbol of the ability of Brazilian athletes and perhaps of the vibrancy of Brazilian culture more broadly. Something even more complex happens when someone who is not a member of the team, perhaps not even a soccer player, purchases and wears a reproduction of Pelé's jersey. Fans do so in order to suggest some connection between themselves, the iconic footballer, and the attitudes and abilities he represents.

Advertising often encourages this sort of mystical connection to products by suggesting that the purchase of goods can provide status or well-being. When a McDonald's ad proclaims, "You deserve a break today," it seeks to turn the act of buying fast food into an expression of self-worth. Ads for luxury goods, whether cars or *couture*, often imply that a primary reason for purchasing these products is the statement they make about your success, sophistication, or social standing. Other identities are also expressed in this way. For several generations the iconic image of the hero of the Cuban revolution, Che Guevara, has been emblazoned on posters and T-shirts. By purchasing and displaying the image, people who may otherwise live entirely conventional lives claim a connection to a revolutionary spirit.

One criticism of consumption is that it substitutes possession for experience and in doing so it promises things it cannot deliver. Just as buying sports paraphernalia connects the non-athlete to the status and assumed values of the athlete, owning an elegant home in a privileged community makes a claim of stability and status, even if the purchaser may be mortgaged to the hilt and in danger of foreclosure.

Similar arguments are often made about the fans of popular culture. By "consuming" action films, romance novels, or super hero comic books, the audience builds a connection with these narratives and images. This is not a new idea. Sigmund Freud (1908) saw the adventure stories and popular romances of his day as an escapist form of wish fulfillment in which the reader identifies with the hero who achieves erotic and material successes beyond that which are possible for the reader. Freud assumed that the consumption of these stories was rooted in a wish for satisfaction that was lacking in the reader's life. So, for example, reading romance novels served as a kind of shared daydream in which an audience dissatisfied with their own romantic lives identified with the heroine's romantic trials and ultimate success.

Consumption is a part of religious life when one buys a book by a spiritual teacher, pays for a child to attend a religious school, or purchases a statue of the Buddha. This attitude also seems to be at work when someone assumes that individual practices, beliefs, images, and icons can be disconnected from the integrated system of belief and practice that they are a part of and repurposed in individualistic religious projects. Within the system of consumption, the objects, practices, and narratives substitute for the experience. Thus, in the consumption of religion it is not necessary to read the book, for the child to pay attention, or for you to meditate on the Buddha for some religious end to be served. It appears that merely owning a Tibetan prayer bowl or a Hopi Kachina figure evokes the spiritual power of these objects and incorporates them into one's religious identity (Figure 3.1).

In the sample reflection in Chapter 1, and more fully in *Oprah: The Gospel of an Icon* (2011), Kathryn Lofton demonstrates how this works for the audience of the enormously popular talk show host Oprah Winfrey. Lofton suggests that Winfrey is not merely the moderator of her TV world, but a model of both the eclectic religious identity creation described in Chapter 1 and of the

Figure 3.1 Hopi Kachina figure

balanced and fulfilled life. Bringing Freud's interpretation into conversation with Lofton suggests that Winfrey's life is a fantasy or daydream that satisfies something that is lacking in the lives of her viewers. While the audience may not realistically be able to be like this hugely successful woman, they make an imaginative connection to her by buying the products she recommends. Winfrey speaks, for instance, about the value of keeping a journal of your reflections, in fact she encourages having multiple journals for separate aspects of your life. Lofton suggests that, within the consumption system, even if you do not go to the extent of actually writing in the journals, simply purchasing the elegant blank books and expensive pens that Oprah recommends connects you to this practice and, by extension, to the power and status of Winfrey herself.

Others go further, suggesting that it is not merely that one can consume religion but that consumption itself has become a religious practice and a form of religious meaning. In the wittily titled *The Sacred Santa: Religious Dimensions of Consumer Culture* (2002), Dell deChant traces the rituals, religious figures, and duties of consumption itself as a religious practice. He suggests that the eternal process of acquiring and consuming has become the central source of meaning in American culture. Consumption is, in effect, the national religion, and its central festival is Christmas, shorn of its historic ties to Christianity and focused on the sainted hero of consumption, Santa Claus.

Active and passive consumption

Much of the critique of consumption rests on the assumption that consumers are powerless in the face of the forces that produce the goods and narratives they consume. The argument goes something like this: Once people lived in local communities where there were direct connections between the producers and consumers of culture. People created art and culture for themselves and their neighbors. Their songs, stories, and symbolic goods were deeply connected to the actual struggles and successes of their lives. In this way coal miners sang songs about the difficulty of life in the mines, Japanese painters painted landscapes that reproduced both their misty mountains and a Shinto sensibility about the world, and so forth. However, industrialization and the resulting commercialization of culture led to a disconnection between producers and consumers. Now culture is a product to be reproduced and marketed to distant audiences. In such a system, those who controlled the means of cultural production imposed cultural forms and assumptions on distant and less powerful cultures. Thus, American movies, television, and music not only find an audience around the world, they fill up the commercial media space, leaving no room for the performance of local forms of art and culture. In doing so, they teach cultural norms and values that are often foreign to their international consumers.

It has been argued, for instance, that television is at least partly to blame for the incidence of eating disorders in the Pacific Islands (Becker *et al.* 2002). Local cultures in places like Fiji used to affirm that women and girls could be both big *and* beautiful. Once television arrived in their culture, though, it taught the citizens to aspire to American forms of beauty that made no sense in the context of Polynesian physiology or extant esthetic norms. Examples like this point to the losses inherent in this sort of cultural change and invite reflection on the question of who shapes the images and stories with which audiences engage.

The power of mediated images and narratives is obvious, and viewers in every culture should be attentive to the way that powerful economic, political, and social forces shape the range of choices available. Yet there are reasons to question some of these assumptions. The passive-consumption theory used above treats people as though they are powerless in the face of a media onslaught, suggesting that they simply absorb the values and assumptions that are embedded in the dominant cultural materials available. Is this an accurate understanding of people and of the way they engage with culture and media systems?

Reading and performing culture

The suggestion that consumption inevitably force-feeds attitudes and values into society in some ways misunderstands the complexity of the relationship between people and the cultural texts, images, and objects they employ in expressing their identity. The consumption model thinks of culture in the way that generations of literary scholars once thought about poems and stories. It assumes that the meaning these things convey is set in the text. The author of the text, or in the case of sacred texts perhaps the God or gods at work through the author, is the source of the meaning, and the audience members are the largely passive recipients. Their task is at best to be careful readers who tease out what the author is telling them.

"Reader response criticism" takes exception to the core assumption of this way of thinking about literature. Reader response critics argue that meaning is produced in the act of reading the text. Meaning is not something hidden within the text but created by readers in interaction with the text. Thus, rather than seeking Shakespeare's vision or intent, reader response critics focus on how readers interpret the poems and how audiences experience the plays. They note that individual readers interpret the texts differently at different stages of their lives and that at different periods in history contemporary cultural concerns bring different issues in the text to the forefront. These various readers are often in conversation with each other. Interpretive communities rise up within cultures, focusing in unique ways on the texts and having interpretive conversations with the texts and with each other. Readers bring their own experience of things like love and disappointment, power and prejudice, and gender and race into conversation with the text.

The terms *text* and *reader* are often used as analogies for non-literary experiences. A film can be seen as "text" and the viewer to be "reading" the film; music, too, could be "text" and the listener could "read" the performance. This analogy can be helpful in that it encourages us to think about the way meaning emerges between the object or experience and person taking it in. But the analogy can also lead us astray. In thinking of them as "texts," viewers run the risk of reducing films to their dialog, disregarding the powerful effect the images, editing, and composition can exert on one's experience of a film. Similarly, we fail to get at the full experience of hearing a song if we disregard rhythm, tune, instrumentation, and harmony. Consider alt-rocker Tori Amos's 2001 cover of rapper Eminem's *'97 Bonnie & Clyde*. The two performances could not be more different, though they are drawing from the same lyrics. In the end it is not the words that differentiate the recordings but variations in style, pace, voicing, and so forth evoking vastly different responses in the listener.

Another term connected to approaches that focus on the audience is *reception*. Studies of reception focus on how the text, cultural object, or experience is received by particular audiences. Rather than focusing on the relationship between the author and the text, reception studies look at the relationship between the text and the audience. The reception approach is also applied to non-textual esthetic creation and cultural experience. Just as we can consider what happens when someone reads a text, we can ask what happens when they gaze on a painting or movie, or when they hear a piece of music. Religious texts, images, architecture, and ritual can all be "read" in this way. These approaches recognize that different audiences read or receive the same esthetic experience in different ways. Alongside the question of what these things may have meant to the original audiences, we can explore what they mean to those who "read" them today.

Consider the varied meanings that a building might carry. In the early 300s CE, in the city now called Istanbul, the emperor Constantine had the *Hagia Sophia* or "Church of the Holy Wisdom" built. When the Ottomans conquered the region in 1453, they turned this structure into a mosque, plastering over the Byzantine mosaics of Christian saints. With the establishment of the secular Turkish state in the 1930s, the *Hagia Sophia* was converted to a museum. Its mosaics were uncovered in the hope that the stately building would stand as a symbol of a less warlike interaction of religions. According to the theory at hand, the *Hagia Sophia* could be considered a kind of cultural "text" which was "read" differently by different viewers at different times in history. At the time it was built it would have served for some as a sign that Christianity was now the official religion of the empire, while for Muslims it was a symbol of the repression of their religions. When it became a mosque these relationships were reversed, and the building continued to be a symbol of the religious conflict of the age and region. These meanings of this contested space have changed over time, representing the dominance of two different religions and later the possibility of shared religious space within a common culture. Our location in history, and our own cultural and religious identities, shape the way we interpret this sacred space.

The responses to the controversial film *The Passion of the Christ* provide a more recent demonstration of the variety of meanings that a single work can carry. Mel Gibson, a member of a conservation movement within Roman Catholicism, directed this film about Jesus' arrest, trial, and crucifixion. To deal with the reception of the film requires us to consider both the different interpretations that critics have made of the film and the way those differences were expressed. (For a fuller discussion of the film and the conflict, see Mahan, 2004.)

Even before the film was released it generated wide discussion. Some responded to the film from an esthetic standpoint, considering its value as, simply, a film. For many, though, *The Passion* was an effort to translate the sacred text of their faith into film. Others in the Jewish community regarded the film as anti-Semitic, arguing that it revived long-abandoned arguments that Jews were responsible for the death of Christ. Conservative Catholics and Evangelical Protestants came together to defend *The Passion*. They used their internal media systems to promote the film and rented theaters to provide free screenings. Liberal Christians, on the other hand, disagreed with the film's theological position and its violence. Both sides wrote letters to the newspapers, held ritualized protests, and appropriated images from the film to support their positions (Figure 3.2). Viewing the DVD became, for some Christians, a regular part of preparation for Easter. For a few years there was a cottage industry of books, articles, and public forums through which critics, religious and secular, interpreted this movie.

Prosumption

In making sense of the consumption of religion, reflect on how people interact with the religious objects, images, and narratives they consume. What are they doing when they "consume" a religious film, a sacred building, or some other manifestation of religion?

The actual practice of audiences, fans, and religious practitioners suggests that they are more than passive consumers. They actively engage with the mediated forms of religion and culture. Meaning is created by the activity of readers when they engage with, reflect on, and act in response to the mediated religion

Figure 3.2 The Passion of the Christ demonstrations

and culture they consume. Futurist Alvin Toffler is generally credited with first combining the terms consumption and production to describe the activity of these active readers and receivers (Toffler 1980). Prosumers simultaneously consume the products of mass culture and produce out of it something new and more individual.

Consider the cultural phenomenon of George Lucas's film franchise *Star Wars*. This series of films that began in 1977 explores a mythic conflict between the heroic forces of good (the rebel alliance) and the forces of evil and repression (the empire). However, the *Star Wars* phenomenon is not adequately described by simply recounting the movies. What could be called a "*Star Wars* universe" developed around the films. Official merchandise is licensed that includes action figures and toys, posters, costumes, books, comic books, and on and on. Response to the film takes on a life of its own, a force far beyond Lucas's control. Fans form clubs, gather at conventions, and write their own unofficial *Star Wars* stories. Children play out *Star Wars* fantasies on playgrounds. People produce parodies and also quote the films as a source of encouragement and moral direction. Some even profess to practice "Jediism," a religion based on the belief in the metaphysical guiding power in the film known as "The Force." A quick Web search today reveals dozens of sites related to the films, some of them overtly professing this religious connection to the films and the culture that surrounds them.

Just as we might understand esthetic experience by focusing on the activities of the audience, we can understand religious experience by focusing on the activities of the practitioners. We saw this in the way religious audiences appropriated *The Passion of the Christ* into their discourse and practice. As with the *Star Wars* universe, fans may develop complex practices around popular culture that serve ritual and meaning-making purposes similar to those in religion.

These activities challenge two common assumptions about media and religion. First is the assumption that those who engage with media/religion are mere passive consumers. The examples just given suggest, in contrast, that people may actually be active participants such as when they take up digital narratives in their own projects of individual and group identity. The second assumption being challenged is that digital religion leads to a disembodied identity, that people's engagement in digital religion happens only in the head and therefore contributes to a split between mind and body. The actual practice of these participants, however, suggests that they move fluidly between participation in both digital and "embodied" practices, as when Jews who participate in an online synagogue or digitally visit Jerusalem's Wailing Wall also light Shabbat candles or participate in the Passover meal.

Erica Doss's seminal study of how Elvis fans established "shrines" to the singer and drew on his image and lyrics as a source of comfort and meaning seemed shocking at first (1999). But now it seems commonplace to suggest that secular phenomena can assume sacred status for some people. Scholars explore the way the material of popular culture and the practices of fandom are used in conjunction with or in place of traditional religious elements. The Super Bowl, for instance, could be seen as a religious ritual engaged in by the entire US nation, or as a religion in and of itself, with rules and rituals for its adherents, both players and fans.

Evaluating consumption as a religious practice

Recognizing that these practices of consumption are not as passive as some have suggested, it is still tempting to dismiss them as insubstantial, saying that surely they are not true forms of religion. However, we learn something about the boundaries of religion by attending to how these things are at least like religion. What does it mean when some of these prosumers describe their activity as religion or use religious language to describe it? It is said that the American novelist and humorist Mark Twain (1835–1910) was once asked whether he believed in infant baptism. Twain is supposed to have replied, "Believe in it? Hell, I have seen it done." However we judge the theological coherence of some of these practices, we must acknowledge, as Twain did, that we are aware of real people who regard their own practice as a legitimate form of religion.

Is religion so elastic a term that it encompasses all these variations, or are there distinctions to be made? In a provocative study of religious charlatans, David Chidester examines the way that items in popular culture such as baseball and Coca-Cola, and figures as diverse as South African president Nelson Mandela and People's Temple leader Rev. Jim Jones, whose followers participated in a mass suicide, take on the forms, language and images of religion (2005). Chidester says that American popular culture has been a particularly rich location for such manifestations of the religious. He suggests that even false religion can give sacred structure to life in culture. This is a provocative suggestion, one that seems to expand what we mean by religion.

Some people question the meaning, utility, and value of these new forms of religion. They prefer to define religion more narrowly. In his book on celebrity culture, *Gods Behaving Badly* (2011), British scholar Pete Ward suggests a category that he calls "para-religion." He suggests that, while it is helpful to think of how celebrities are *like* gods and demi-gods, and while the attraction to them is a form of veneration, it is also useful to notice that there is no "church" of celebrity, that this veneration does not unify society as religion is said to do, nor do celebrities connect us to some ongoing chain of meaning. For Ward much of what is being discussed is not religion; rather it is like religion. Religion—or people's ideas about it—provides a sort of analogy for understanding something that is not quite religion. With his discussion of para-religion Ward protects the specialness of religion by excluding practices like the veneration of celebrities or the claiming of special powers for products like Coke. Thus he excludes what could be called "weak" forms of religion that do not fully serve the cultural and individual purposes of religion. Ward's critics argue that the term *religion* should be elastic enough to include both weak and strong expressions of religion, including even ephemeral and inchoate practices. This debate about the boundaries and definitions of religion helps demonstrate more clearly what religion is, and the various things religion is doing in digital culture.

Religion is an organizational category, a term we use to help us think about an incredibly diverse range of practices. In practice no one is "religious" as such; rather, they have particular practices and beliefs that shape their orientation toward life. They understand themselves to be Hindus, Jews, followers of Jim Jones, or perhaps fans of Elvis, or devotees of Coca-Cola. The actual practice of religion in daily life often blurs boundaries between what is and is not theoretically and/or traditionally considered religion.

It is tempting to set the term *religion* aside for what we might think of as more serious forms of spiritual practice. Maybe the veneration of movies and celebrities is simply playing with the forms of religion. Where is the line between play with religion and actual religious practice? Think of Cathleen Falsani, the Evangelical blogger/Dudist priest described in Chapter 2. Her playful engagement with the Coen Brothers character "The Dude" is, along with Evangelical Christianity, integrated into her unique eclectic religious identity.

Transitory communities of practice

Understanding religion in the media age requires attention to both long-established faith communities and emerging forms of practice, some of which may be transitory and some of which may result in established religious institutions. It is less than 40 years after Lucas's first film in the *Star Wars* series, and so it is perhaps too soon to tell whether Jediism will stick or pass out of practice.

That particular expressions of religion are transitory need not mean that they are without meaning or significance. Are the roadside memorials that are common in Hispanic Catholic communities in the American Southwest and the spontaneous public memorials and rituals at places of tragic death insincere or ineffective because they have not resulted in ongoing religious institutions or communities? Similarly, the establishment of physical or digital shrines to dead celebrities, the practices of fans who create their own narratives based on popular material, and the reuse of digital culture in art and activism can be understood as means of establishing and expressing the religious self.

Discussion questions

1   The author suggests that the Internet provides digital spaces within which people can practice religion. Do you agree or disagree, and why? What sort of religious practice is happening online today? How is this like and different from religion offline?

2   The chapter argues that in capitalist cultures consumption becomes an expression of identity and can be considered a source of religious meaning. Describe examples of this.

3   A common critique of consumption is that consumption is largely a passive activity through which powerful forces impose identity on consumers. What do you find compelling about that argument? What counter-argument does the chapter develop? Do you find it compelling? What examples do you see?

4   Can celebrities or forms of popular culture take on religious meaning for people? On what grounds would you argue that this is religion? Is it helpful or problematic to make a distinction between *true* religion and *para-religion*? Why?

5   The reflections that follow consider examples of online religion. What do the religious *mommy bloggers* studied by Whitehead suggest about religious authority and community in today's media culture? What do the studies of online *puja* that Chiou examines suggest about the meaning of place, ritual and pilgrimage in religion today?

References

Becker, A.E., Burwell, R.A., Gilman, S.E., Herzog, D.B., and Hamburg, P. (2002) "Eating Behaviours and Attitudes following Prolonged Television Exposure among Ethnic Fijian Adolescent Girls," *The British Journal of Psychiatry*, 180: 509–14.

Chidester, David (2005) *Authentic Fakes: Religion and American Popular Culture*, Berkeley: University of California Press.

deChant, Dell (2002) *The Sacred Santa: Religious Dimensions of Consumer Culture*, Cleveland, OH: Pilgrim Press.

Doss, Erika (1999) *Elvis Culture: Fans, Faith, and Image*, Lawrence: University Press of Kansas.

Freud, Sigmund (1908) "Creative Writers and Day Dreaming," in Peter Gay, ed. (1989) *The Freud Reader*, New York: W.W. Norton & Company.

Lofton, Kathryn (2011) *Oprah: The Gospel of an Icon*, Berkley: University of California Press.

Mahan, Jeffrey (2004) "Talking about *The Passion of the Christ*," *Lectionary Homiletics*, Vol. XV, No. 4: 5–6, June/July.

Toffler, Alvin (1980) *The Third Wave*, New York: William Morrow and Company.

Ward, Pete (2011) *Gods Behaving Badly: Media, Religion, and Celebrity Culture*, Waco, TX: Baylor University Press.

Reflection

Mom blogs and the religion of everyday life

Deborah Whitehead

A figure of 14 percent of all US mothers belong to the category of "mom bloggers," broadly defined as "women who have at least one child in their household and have read or contributed to a blog in the past 30 days." According to a recent study, the average age of a mom blogger is 37, and they are statistically better educated, wealthier, and more politically involved and socially aware than the average American mother. There are currently approximately 4 million "mommy blogs" in the United States.[1] Religious or faith-based mom blogs add religion and spirituality to the rich mix of topics considered by mom bloggers: pregnancy, parenting, marriage/family life, homemaking, crafting, cooking, finances/frugal living, etc. Evangelical Protestants and Mormons dominate the religious mom blog category, with a growing chorus of voices from Muslim, Jewish, Wiccan, pagan/earth spirituality, and atheist communities as well.

The popularity of mom blogs suggests two things about religion in digital space. First, just as mom blogs have revolutionized motherhood by making regular moms the authorities about parenting (rather than ivory tower academics and male doctors), religious mom bloggers constitute emerging authoritative voices on religion. These women write about religion out of their own everyday life experiences in highly personal and accessible ways. Evangelical Christian Angie Smith (http://angiesmithonline.com) began her blog in 2008 while pregnant with her fourth child, who suffered from fatal birth defects. The blog became a way to process her grief and reflect theologically through this painful experience, building a vibrant community of readers in the process. She came to see her blog as a narrative of her daughter Audrey's short life and also of God working through her experiences to minister to others, so that her readers too may "become a part of the story that God is weaving us into."[2] Mormon Stephanie Nielson (http://nieniedialogues.blogspot.com) has blogged since 2005 about how her faith gives meaning and purpose to her life as a wife and mother of five. Her readership and sense of purpose for her blog changed dramatically after she suffered burns over 80 percent of her body in an airplane crash in 2008. When asked in a 2011 interview why her blog appealed to so many readers all over the world (nearly 5.5 million), she said:

I've had several emails from people who are atheists and they say, "I sure feel something when I read your blog." It's really brought different faiths from all over together. It's just a story of faith and hope and a love story. There are different people with different ideals and faiths but this story just resonates because it's a story of God's hand. What it is is that they feel the Spirit. I'm working through His hands. I'm doing everything he tells me to do and I don't claim any of it. I'm hoping to get people to come to Christ and be baptized. I hope that through my words and my tragedy turned miracle turned wonderful story that people will see that there's a God, that's all.[3]

This quote reveals the second way that religious mom blogs signify in digital spaces: they are a vehicle for personal religious testimony, particularly in traditions such as evangelical Protestantism and Mormonism, where testifying is a central part of one's faith and where blogging is encouraged as a way of giving testimony and spreading the faith. Both of these mom bloggers have developed audiences far beyond the blogosphere because of their powerful testimonies. Smith has launched a women's ministry through her blog, authoring three books and speaking at conferences across the United States. Nielson's blog proudly features links to the Church of Jesus Christ of Latter-Day Saints' official website, teachings, and conferences, and she offers to send readers a free copy of the Book of Mormon. She has been featured in the "Mormon Message" ad campaign, as well as on the *Today Show* and *Oprah*, and has authored a best-selling book about her recovery and her positive attitude toward life.

Offering theological reflections out of the material of daily life, religious mom bloggers constitute a growing network of emerging authoritative voices about religion in digital space.

Notes

1 Sam Laird, "The Rise of the Mommy Blogger," Mashable.com, May 8, 2012. Available at: http://mashable.com/2012/05/08/mommy-blogger-infographic/; full report from Scarborough available at: www.scarborough.com/fs248584273/Scarborough-Mom-Bloggers-Infographic.pdf; accessed March 30, 2013.
2 Angie Smith, "The Beginning of the Story … ," Angie Smith/Bring the Rain blog, January 12, 2008. Available at: http://angiesmithonline.com/2008/01/the-beginning-of-the-story, accessed April 13, 2013.
3 Stephanie Nielson, Interview, Conversations: Stephanie Nielson—Episode 26, Mormon Channel, available at www.mormonchannel.org/conversations/26?lang=eng, accessed April 13, 2013.

Reflection

Online *puja* and *puja* online: believing and practicing in a digital world

Grace Chiou

Hinduism is a complex and sensually rich religious practice that developed in the Indian subcontinent. It is known in the West as the source of yoga, for the concept of karma, and for its multiple deities and the rituals through which they are venerated. This ancient tradition provides a multifaceted case study in the mediation of religion online and offline and the resulting transitions in religious practice and authority.

Puja is a Hindu worship ritual which involves making a number of offerings to a deity. Millions of Hindus perform this ritual regularly, which includes *darshan*, worshiping an image or *murti* which is not understood as a likeness of a deity but as the god or goddess manifested and embodied, "deity itself taken form" (Eck 1996: 38). Traditionally *puja* was performed in the home, or at temples, and often was part of a pilgrimage to historic Hindu sites. Today, a number of Hindu temples or teachers have responded to the digital age by offering online resources to facilitate the performance of *puja*. This happens in two ways.

First, when *puja* is practiced online, one gazes into the eyes of the *murti* on a screen rather than at a temple or shrine. While online *puja* may offer a different sensory experience, lacking the smells of incense or taste of food offerings of *puja* rituals conducted at home or in a temple, the online format retains the emphasis and importance of "seeing" and visuality that are rooted in the Hindu religious tradition. Diana Eck (1996) points to the "power and importance of 'seeing' ... not only must the gods keep their eyes open, but so must we in order to make contact with them, to reap their blessings and to know their secrets." Online *puja* has occurred for more than a decade and if you do a Web search for "online *puja*" you will find many websites that have posted *murtis* (Figure 3.3).

Devotees gaze at the image on the Internet and see animated components of traditional *puja*. One can select options for honor offerings such as water, leaves, flowers, or incense.

Alternatively, at some temple sites a devotee orders and pays online for the ritual to be completed on their behalf at a physical temple by a *pujari* or priest (Scheifinger 2010). Purchasing *puja* to be done on one's behalf has been a traditional practice, and the concept of *puja* online is an extension of worship practiced on one's behalf which allows the diaspora

Figure 3.3 Puja with computer

to reconnect with "sacred homelands" (Helland 2007). The Web's anonymity expands worship possibilities to non-Hindus in cyberspace as the inner sanctum of a physical temple is typically off limits to non-Hindus or non-Indians (Scheifinger 2010).

In addition, any seeker could either watch a live stream of *puja* or read *puja* instructions written in English (Herman 2010). Thus, both online *puja* and *puja* online are made accessible to non-Hindus via the Web. Scheifinger also discusses how *puja* online has altered hierarchical authority between temple authorities and *pujaris* and also between the *puja* providers and the temple. Whether practicing *puja* digitally on an app or website, or ordered online, the Internet has broadened the social accessibility of *puja* but posed offline challenges whereby traditional authorities are bypassed and *puja* providers are exercising authority.

References

Eck, D. (1996) *Darsan: Seeing the Divine Image in India*, 2nd edition, New York: Columbia University Press.

Helland, Christopher (2007) "Diaspora on the Electronic Frontier: Developing Virtual Connections with Sacred Homelands," *Journal of Computer-Mediated Communication*, 12.

Herman, P.K. (2010) "Seeing the Divine through Windows—Online Darshan and Virtual Religious Experience," *Online—Heidelberg Journal of Religions on the Internet*, 4(1): 151–78.

Scheifinger, H. (2010) "Internet Threats to Hindu Authority: *Puja*-ordering Websites and the *Kalighat* Temple," *Asian Journal of Social Science*, 38: 636–56.

Part 2

Religion in the midst of change

Part 1 focused on religion as a matter of personal identity and explored ways that individuals construct their religious identities, often by drawing on ideas and practices from multiple traditions and sources. Part 2 shifts our focus from individual religious practice to examine how established and emerging religious authorities, institutions, and communities use and respond to media change.

One might ask whether it is relevant to focus on organized religion in the digital age. Many of the likely readers of this book live in regions or countries where increasing numbers of people do not practice within traditional religious communities and, when polled, many of them assert no religious belief. In some places, perhaps most notably the Nordic countries, people have not done so for generations. This is not only the case in northern Europe. Sociologists of religion have come to call the Pacific Northwest of the United States the "none zone" because, when surveyed about their religious affiliation, more people say "none" than in any other part of the country (Killen and Silk 2004). Examples like these lead us to ask whether religion has gone away or is in the process of dying out. Is society becoming increasingly secular? At least in some places, this seems to be a convincing possibility. Yet organized religion continues to be important to the identity of numerous people and a force in many societies. Understanding religion today requires understanding of the more individualistic expressions explored in Part 1 and the power and influence of established and emerging religions. Accordingly, Part 2 gives attention to the way established religions adapt to, participate in, and respond to changing media cultures.

Chapter 4: Old and new media considers what makes "new media" new. Pre-digital media systems maintained a clear distinction between the author and the audience. Thus they privileged certain perspectives and locations by magnifying and privileging the voice of authors embedded in a cultural system. New, fairly inexpensive digital media systems provide vastly greater interactivity, making it possible for more people to initiate media conversations. They enable multiple voices and multiple centers of religious and cultural authority. By enabling a wider range of voices and faster and more regular interaction between "readers," they challenge the distinction between author and audience.

Chapter 5: Stability and change examines how the practices, theologies, and forms of authority of traditional religious communities change in response to changes in the larger media culture that they inhabit. Established religion changes in reaction to new forms of media, and new forms of media make spaces for emerging religious sensibilities.

Chapter 6: Organized religion in the age of digital media further considers how established religions adopt and resist media change and the impact of those decisions. It goes on to explore how media can provide a location for emerging religion.

Reference

Killen, Patricia O'Connell and Silk, Mark eds. (2004) *Religious and Public Life in the Pacific Northwest: The None Zone*, Walnut Creek, CA: Rowan & Littlefield Publishers, Inc.

4 Old and new media

Key ideas

- The "old media" systems such as print and network television confirmed the authority of traditional political, esthetic, and religious leaders by amplifying their voices and excluding alternative voices.
- New media are best thought of as interactive spaces rather than merely as collections of easily accessible texts. These spaces can be locations for religious practice, and paying attention to what is happening in them helps to explain changes in religion that are simultaneously taking place in physical settings.
- Interactivity is the key attribute that distinguishes today's digital *new media* from old. This interactivity challenges traditional centers of authority by enabling a vast range of new voices. The ability to have one's own voice and to interact with multiple religious and esthetic sources are basic resources for the construction of unique individual religious identities.

This chapter considers two questions. First, how are today's *new media* different from old media. Second, how and why is religion changing in relationship to these changes in media? Earlier chapters suggested that religion has always been mediated and that religion adapts to changes in mediation. What then is distinctive about the media change in what is often called the digital era, and how is religious practice adapting to these changes?

Defining *new media*

The term *new media* has at least two distinct meanings.

First, every medium was at some point new. New forms of communication inevitably challenge the assumptions about communication and culture of their day and make possible new media and religious practices. The development of the printing press and the resulting rise in literacy discussed in earlier chapters provides an obvious example of this. It is possible to go much earlier in human history in thinking about the impact of the development of new media. Consider language itself as a medium of communication. Presumably the earliest uses of language were expressions of fear and desire, requests for fire, food, shelter, and sex. But, language also made it possible to articulate emotions, to recall the past and imagine the future, to tell stories and to begin to speak of spirits and realities beyond the immediate and physical realm. You can think of this in terms of human evolution but also see it in the life of an individual. The early speech acts of a child developing language skills might name those on whom the child is dependent, "Mama" or "Dada." Soon, "no" and "yes" give the child some control over her environment. As her language skills develop, this medium of communication becomes a place of play, of story, and of self-expression. Even today, as your composition professor reminds you, there is power in deepening the sophistication of your language.

The development of new forms of media and the practices that grow up around them draws our attention to their possibilities and limits. Again we can think of this in terms of individual development as well as within human history. The child's maturing language skills allow her to express her feelings and personality in new ways. When she is in the midst of developing these skills, the adults around her are particularly aware of the implications of these developments. Later they may take for granted that she can speak, and they probably think little about what language adds and perhaps subtracts from her life. What is true in the development of the child is true for human communities as well. When people first discover and develop a new form of communication, they are extra attentive to how the medium is being used and to what we might be losing and gaining with it.

In this sense, a medium is new in the period when its basic forms and capacities are emerging and when people are first thinking about its influence on human communities. New media allow new forms of ritual, new ways to express belief and articulate a religious self. The relationship of religion, media, and culture is particularly evident as religion negotiates media change, for, once the mediations of religion are established, people become acculturated to them and they seem largely invisible.

Second, today the term new media refers to digital media and the Internet; and to the ease with which it is possible to sample, comment on and incorporate material from one form or message to another; and to the practices that have grown up around these technologies.

Summarizing the work of Lev Manovitch (2001), Heidi Campbell identifies five distinctive technical characteristics of new media. First, they are *digital*, and therefore they can be mathematically manipulated with computers. Second, information (words, sounds, images) is organized in *modules* that can be manipulated individually and organized into larger units. Third, much of the process of creation and manipulation of information is *automated*, serving to increase speed and happening with limited human intervention. Fourth, these modules are infinitely *variable*, allowing for multiple versions of these new media objects. The fifth characteristic is *transcoding*: new media objects are easily translated from one format to another (Campbell 2010: 9).

Commenting on the social function and ethical implications of these new digital technologies and on the practices that develop around them, Lynn Schofield Clark notes four social characteristics of digital media. They are *persistent*: once uploaded to the Internet, information is difficult to remove. Second, they are constantly *changeable*: easily copied, altered, and reposted. Third, they are *scalable*: what is posted can be reposted, making it easy for something to "go viral." And fourth, digital media are easily *searchable*: for good or ill, whatever is digitized and put on the Internet is easily recoverable (Clark 2012: 7).

A college or university website provides an example of a new media location that reflects these elements. It is a digital creation likely combining text, images, and perhaps sounds. Different departments and individuals provide digital information, which is then manipulated by the school's marketing department and the Web designer to highlight key terms that will drive potential students or donors to the website. The information is easily changed and expanded to reflect changes in how the school wants to present itself. Transcoding makes it possible to embed photos of the football team, a recording of the commencement speaker, a faculty member's blog, and admissions office forms in the site. Because the information is modular (it is part of the whole, while remaining distinct), it can be easily changed. If a faculty member wins the Nobel Prize, information about her work can be added with little effort. And this modular structure gives the site depth; from the homepage you can click on *Academics*, then on the *French Department*, then on the homepage of your French instructor *Professeur Trudeau*, and then on the professor's *e-mail* to explain why you will be out of town during mid-terms.

New media cannot be fully understood by focusing only on such institutional sites. In a world of transcodable and scalable new media, the college cannot fully control its digital presence. Others also have access to new media in ways that shape how your school is presented to the world. Googling the school's name will pull up student reviews of the school and of individual faculty members. A reputation as a "party school" might emerge in students' Facebook pages. In the late 1990s, during a time of conflict on my campus, protesting students maintained a counter-website to the school's official site expressing their complaints about the administration. More benignly, during a recent spring program of graduating student skits, my "official school photo" and those of several colleagues were downloaded and manipulated to comic effect. An understanding of new media needs to include seeing how the accessibility of these tools and media spaces enables the development of such personal, though hardly private, media practices.

It is not simply the technological marvel of the digital world that constitutes new media. The term also refers to the institutional and individual human practices that grow up around this technology and create new media cultures. To understand media cultures requires understanding both the esthetic forms available and the economic and political systems that control access to the means of production.

Access and power

The question of who is making use of the possibilities of new media raises questions of access and therefore of power. The forms of communication that preceded the digital age, such as newspaper and book publishing and radio and television broadcasting, were expensive and were organized and controlled by corporate or government interests. These economic and esthetic systems will be more fully discussed in later chapters; here it is enough to note that access was limited by the costs of publishing and broadcasting and by the technical complexity which required particular skills and training.

Television provides an example of how economics and access shape a medium. Before cable and satellite distribution systems there were a limited number of outlets. Broadcast quality video was expensive and complicated, requiring skilled technicians. In order to spread the costs, broadcasters sought the widest possible audience. This shaped the kinds of stories that were told and led to the development of organized systems, whether governmental systems such as the British Broadcasting Corporation or corporate networks like ABC, CBS, and NBC in the United States. Thus, a fairly limited group of producers, advertisers, and regulators representing a few established centers of political and economic power controlled distribution and consequently the content of the programming seen by viewers. The vast majority of people were consumers rather than producers of media, and they had little influence on the content and structures of the media they consumed. In the midst of the civil rights and anti-war movements of the late 1960s and early 1970s, activist musician Gil Scott-Heron called attention to the limitations of the news media in what became an iconic song of the era, "The Revolution Will Not Be Televised." In the song, still available on YouTube, Scott-Heron was commenting on the way that a few powerful economic centers controlled the key media outlets of the day and, as a result, influenced conventional political discourse. The song charges that these controlling bodies were missing the significant social changes going on at the time because the changes were happening in places largely invisible to the mainstream media.

One striking change brought about by digital technology has been the breakdown of the established centers of media power and the expansion of the range of available voices. Before cable and satellite television, American viewers chose what they would consume from among the programs offered by three controlling national television networks. Today, the networks compete with hundreds of programming sources, with video games, programming on the Internet, and amateur videos that may have been shot on someone's phone and distributed on the Internet. Not only do people have a wider range of choices, they have access to more interactive media, allowing them to manipulate and respond to the images and narratives of popular culture. For many this blurs the line between producer and consumer.

The same point can be made about music production. In the old-media world of records and radio, the goal of a new band or individual performer was to sign a contract with an established record company and get their music played on the radio in order to drive sales. Consumers were dependent on the record companies to recognize and record performers and on radio to introduce them to new styles and artists. How different is the music world today! Digital technologies have changed the way that music is produced and consumed. Inexpensive recording and mixing technologies mean that artists can produce their own recordings. They develop websites, and use social media to develop a following. Some artists now think that record companies are an unnecessary anachronism, while others combine old and new means of production, promotion, and distribution. Here again, the distinction between consumer and producer breaks down as listeners download what they want; compile their own mixes of artists and styles; sample, pirate, and parody existing music; and use sampled bits as background for their own creative projects.

The political implications of the spread of voices in the media are obvious. Repressive governments seek to control the media, particularly in times of unrest. But social media like Facebook, Twitter, and texting are much more difficult to control than traditional forms of media. In 2011, during what came to be called the "Arab Spring," people in Egypt, Libya, Morocco, and other nations of the region took to the streets and in some cases took up arms, demanding more democratic governments. New media made it possible for this revolution to be televised, sometimes by international news media from Fox News to Al Jazeera, and sometimes by cell phone videos posted and forwarded around the world. New media have not simply covered the revolution; they have been part of it (Figure 4.1). Social media were a key tool in fomenting and organizing the protests. This has not been without consequence. In Egypt, Google executive Wael Ghonim was arrested for his role in organizing Facebook resistance that led to actions in the streets.

In recognizing the democratization of media worlds, it is important not to overlook the way in which governments and corporations continue to shape

Figure 4.1 Egyptian protester streams a demonstration via Skype

and control large segments of the contemporary media world. Repressive governments seek to control access to the Internet, and corporate media interests continue to influence what is covered in news and entertainment media. The economic systems through which independent writers, musicians, and journalists will make a living are still emerging. Exciting as the new media options are, the loss of the systems that established and maintained journalistic and esthetic standards has resulted in the distribution of work that is often sloppy and narcissistic. It has, however, also allowed people access to new voices and those reflecting non-dominant cultures.

Religion and new media

Just as politics and the music and news industries have adapted to the culture of media, religion also responds to the possibilities and limitations of the digital environment. To understand religion today it is necessary to pay attention to how religious institutions, communities, and individuals resist and adapt to media change as part of negotiations of theological and political power.

When religious figures or institutions learn to use a new or changing medium, they grow in social power. If new leaders emerge who are quicker than established leaders to understand and adapt to the possibilities of emerging media they gain an advantage in the marketplace of ideas and practices. As these leaders develop new practices that take advantage of the potential of new media, religion changes in ways that may be striking or quite subtle.

Established religious leaders and institutions tend to trust existing means of communication and doubt that new forms will adequately express their tradition. Only after a period of resistance to media change will they adapt to new media and it often takes time to live into the implications of these new technologies. Today, for example, both the Pope and the Dalai Lama have Twitter accounts. When they, or perhaps others in their names, tweet, scores of people read the message. However, the change from old to new media is not simply a shift in communication platforms. Top-down systems of authority are challenged by a media culture that enables immediate response, critique, and conversation. When multiple voices have access to the media of the day, authority is flattened. Where once a few authorized religious voices were legitimated by their access to, and control of, the limited number of media outlets, today many competing voices have access.

Social media provide entrepreneurial space within which new religious practices develop and new religious leaders emerge. Access to new media allows these emerging leaders to develop a voice and a following without having to move slowly through the ranks of established religious communities. People in roles such as *webmaster* or *blogger* can quickly amass religious influence when they use their roles to model and interpret religious belief and practice. Tensions arise when these emerging voices interact with more traditional sources of religious authority. Community becomes more diffuse and practice more idiosyncratic. While religious authorities can be part of the conversation in new media spaces, they can't easily control the conversation. Their voices compete with others to set the agenda, interpret traditions, and prescribe appropriate religious practice. New media forms like Twitter and Facebook are conversational; they are structured to encourage comment and support. It would be naïve to assume that, by learning to tweet or maintaining Facebook pages, Roman Catholic bishops could reclaim the role they once had in the one-directional world of official Catholic publications and news outlets. The new media spaces require new forms of leadership.

It is not simply that new leaders come to the forefront in emerging media cultures. Today, religious practice may be changing in ways that alter how people relate to leaders or even their need for leaders. One form of traditional religious leadership was authorship. Leaders produced texts that became sacred, other leaders interpreted those texts, developed theologies, or wrote tracts intended to convert non-believers, and published commentary on contemporary culture from religious perspectives. Followers read these religious works, weighed their meaning and authority, and attempted to apply their teachings to daily life. Part of today's changing media culture is seen in the new Web-based interactive media that amplify the spaces for debate, such as chat rooms, Facebook, Web pages, Second Life, and so forth. While the audiences for old media were active as readers and responded in a variety of ways, the texts themselves were fixed. New media are introducing new levels of interactivity that challenge the distinction between producers and consumers of media. When Wiki-like texts are under constant revision, when readers sample them, use them in new contexts, and comment on and change them it is difficult to say who "the" author of a text is.

These new media developments lead to several new understandings of leadership. First, people are likely to follow multiple leaders and participate in overlapping communities, such as by following many religious leaders or celebrities on Twitter, rather than belonging to fixed communities with a single leader. Second, when possession of charisma and access to media are sources of authority, those whose authority rests on education and official position wield less persuasion. Third, in a culture of choice, individuals tend to think of themselves as having the authority to author their own lives. They draw from multiple sources without conceding to any single source the authority to direct their lives. Effective leaders in such a media culture may offer vision and direction, but they cannot be authoritarian. New language is needed to describe and interpret religion in new media spaces. In the remainder of this chapter we will consider two terms that help serve this function.

Networked identity

Network signifies identity that is constructed and expressed through participation in multiple overlapping groups rather than in a single social location. Though the term is not unique to her, I am indebted to Heidi Campbell's (2012) discussion of the idea of "networked societies" and "networked religion." The rise of networks points to a shift in the predominant way that people relate to each other and express identity in contemporary Western culture. Certainly, people have long participated in communities that we might describe as networks such as the family, the village or neighborhood, the religious community, and the workplace. But the term *networked identity*, as used here, refers to this multiplicity in combination with the resistance to the idea that some single setting is the primary center of identity in late modernity.

Internet-based social media provide a helpful image of networked relationships. The ability to sample and edit (transcoding), easily putting things in new relationships, is a metaphor for this new way of relating. Many people think of their own identity as being like a digital text constructed from the images and information they have gathered from multiple networks within which they function. My own Facebook page provides an illustration of a networked relationship. In pre-networked society I kept my various roles distinct, presenting myself in some places primarily in terms of my role in the family, in other places in terms of my relationships with professional colleagues and students, in others in terms of my religious community, and in others in connection to those who share my passion for the movies or for bicycle racing. On Facebook these elements are simultaneously revealed. The different parts of my identity interact there, so that my Facebook friends from one network see me in relationship to others. Further, I am drawn into their networks, where I can see on their pages the posts of people with whom I have no other contact.

The significance of networks becomes clear if we contrast them with more linear, located, traditional forms of relationship. Identity and relationship were once understood as essentially fixed matters of one's location within hierarchically maintained institutions such as the family, the church, and the nation-state, and through social constructions like race, class, and gender. People largely inherited these identities, and changing them meant converting from one social location to another. In the West, for instance, "family" traditionally referred to the biological nuclear family organized around its male head. It was the primary source of identity and one left it only through marriage, which created another nuclear family. Today, the concept of family is more fluid. People gather in a variety of households and partnerships that may be lasting or transitory. They may claim as family people to whom they are not related by blood and with whom they do not cohabitate. Varying understandings of authority and equality guide these relationships. In networked society one moves more easily in and out of various forms of "family." Further, the family is but one of the many networks within which people perform their identity.

In a traditional system a person was one predetermined thing and could not easily become another. In the context of religion, the person was part of a particular tradition, say Judaism, and part of a particular cultural expression of that tradition such as a progressive British synagogue or an ultra-Orthodox Israeli community. The person's race, class, and gender as defined by the hierarchy of her tradition further shaped how she expressed that religious identity. Networked religious communities, on the other hand, "function as loose social networks with varying levels of religious affiliation and commitment" (Campbell 2012: 83). Identity is not simple in networked cultures. Rather than occupying a single social location, individuals build a complex web of interconnection that links them to other people and communities. Their web is both personal and a part of the larger web of network society. Campbell writes, "The network image helps us examine the complex interplay and negotiations occurring between individuals and the community, new and old sources of authority, and public and private identities" (2012: 65).

Today, people practice religion and organize their beliefs through such overlapping networks. Again, contrasting this notion to the non-networked alternative helps make its significance clear. In the past, religious identity and belief was largely fixed. Most often one inherited the religion of one's parents or wholly broke with that tradition and adopted a different religious tradition. One belonged to a particular synagogue, congregation, mosque, or temple and practiced in ways that were culturally and theologically normative for that community. In contrast, in a religious network one transcodes, creating religious identity from multiple relationships. Membership and orthodoxy are less important to people in transcoded, networked relationships. These people may relate with varying degrees of intensity to several local religious communities, they may incorporate ideas or practices from teachers outside their tradition, and they may have personalized religious rituals and images. As Campbell put it, "It may be that in the future we will think of religious practices more in terms of the networks of interactions that produce them than in relationship to formal communities" (personal communication 2012).

A theological school colleague once commented that a Christian cannot fly Buddhist prayer flags. For him, the differences between Christian and Buddhist understandings of the religious life and its goals cannot easily be resolved. These religions' views on crucial matters such as what is sacred, the goals of the religious life, and the way people should practice their religion are fundamentally different and the professor argued that religious identity is established in choosing one over the other. This perspective is rooted in the assumption that religion and religious identity should cohere around a theological center. However, for the networked practitioner who simultaneously flies Buddhist prayer flags and worships a Christian God such clarity of center does not appear to be the goal. This person has cultivated her identity more through interactive practice than through the articulation of intellectually coherent systems of thought. Social media both illustrate and facilitate this networked way of relating, part of a larger pattern of modern social change that includes such things as geographic and social mobility and the rise of the individual.

Third spaces

The idea of *third spaces* is another concept that is emerging to describe religion in new media cultures. The phrase captures the geographic analogy through which people think about new media. Consider the term *online*. A verb we often use with this term is *go*, as in "I need to go online to check the movies that are playing." Using *online* in this way implies that it is a place we can visit. It is a space, and in this space media cultures are at work.

Hoover and Echchaibi (2012) provide a helpful elaboration on this concept. They point out that the term *third spaces* evolved from the sociological notion of "third places" that exist between the purely private space of the home and the public spaces of work and government. These are places where people gather and interact, such as clubs, bars, and cafes. In these venues activity is not purely personal, it serves a social good without being organized and directed.

In digital culture there are virtual third spaces where people hang out and relate. These third spaces are shared, so they are not entirely private, yet they are not controlled by traditional religious institutions and authorities. In the language of religious studies these are locations of "lived religion," where people perform their religious lives. What the term *third spaces* points to is the "in-between-ness" of these spaces. Hoover and Echchaibi write that the third spaces of religion exist somewhere "beyond institution (churches, mosques, denominations, faith groups) as the first space and individual practices as the second group" (Hoover and Echchaibi 2012: 9). In third spaces religion happens outside the institutional, yet in ways that are not purely individual. Chapter 1 discussed Hoover's assertion that the contemporary religious task is one of individual identity construction that draws on institutionalized and inherited practices and beliefs but is not contained within a particular religious institution or tradition. The idea of third spaces expands on this insight by demonstrating that religious identity construction happens in conversation with others.

The informal third spaces where digital religion is practiced are often measured against embodied institutional spaces and then judged on the basis of whether they are an adequate substitution for embodied or institutionalized religion. Hoover and Echchaibi disagree with this approach. They write, "We do not claim they are in any way the 'same thing' [as institutionalized religion] ... . [Third spaces] are in their effect 'emergent cultures' ... fluid spaces of practice through which cultural power can be articulated, grasped and (potentially) deployed" (Hoover and Echchaibi 2012: 12).

Drawing on post-colonial discourse (see Bhahba 1994), Hoover and Echchaibi argue that third spaces can be spaces of resistance to dominant beliefs and practices. Where religion has been a partner in oppression, their between-ness allows third spaces to sometimes be places "of disruption and invention ... that ... arguably unsettles the singularity of dominant power narratives and opens up new avenues of identification and enunciation" (Hoover and Echchaibi: 14). These third spaces are not the locations of purely individual and perhaps self-indulgent play with the religious but potentially creative sites of liberative practice. In third spaces new ideals, claims, identities, and solidarities can be articulated that resist dominant voices, practices, and beliefs.

One such online third space discussed is PostSecret, a Web-based project in which people anonymously express some secret on an often handmade or modified post card. This project is a location for confession, a practice typically thought of as religious. Each week images of elaborately constructed postcards are posted on the website. Some are traditional confessions of wrongdoing; others express secret personal trauma or emotional pain.

Once one might have gone into the anonymity of the church confessional and relied on the priest to pronounce God's forgiveness. By way of PostSecret, however, people are able to confess to the unseen community of those who visit the site without the seeming need for official confirmation of forgiveness. The process of posting has a ritualistic quality, and there is also a ritual in following the posts. Visitors come to the online site to peruse the sometimes troubling, sometimes beautiful cards. PostSecret demonstrates the blurring of the boundary between online and offline. Some followers gather in small groups to read and discuss the cards, and the founder of PostSecret appears at public events, often on college campuses, to discuss the site.

In summary, this chapter suggests that the history of religion is always rooted in the story of its resistance and adaptation to changing forms of media. New media provide spaces for the development of new religious leaders and communities both within and outside of established communities of practice. These changes within religion reflect broader cultural changes brought about by access to new digital and online technologies. Today the access to these new media technologies that so easily segment, save, manipulate, and integrate information contributes to a sense that religious identity is itself constructed from multiple sources, and new religious communities and associations may be transitory or lasting.

Discussion questions

1 The term *new media* is used in two different ways in the chapter. How does any new medium interact with religion? What evidence do we have of religions changing in response to new forms of media? What is distinctive about the digital developments that are called new media today? What new possibilities do they open, and what challenges do established religions face in today's new media culture?

2 What is meant by the term *digital* media? What are the characteristics of the digital, and how is it changing media practices? The chapter suggests that people come to think of their own religious identity as a digital construction. Do you see evidence of this in the chapter or in your own observations? What are the implications of such a digital religious identity?

3 What evidence is there that religion and media were at work in the protests and uprisings that are often called the Arab Spring? How have social media and/or the news media been part of these social and political developments?

4 The chapter suggests that established religions have tended to resist new forms of media. Why is this the case? What challenges do established religious leaders and institutions face when media cultures change?

What possibilities for religious change and innovation do new forms of media create?

5 In her reflection on a religious video game Wagner suggests that, while patterned loosely on biblical narratives, the game and similar "first person shooter" games make the player a god-like savior. Is this "just entertainment," or are there religious and political consequences to such game playing? Does playing such games shape the way people think about real world religious conflicts, and how they imagine intervening in them?

6 In a reflection that encompasses both senses of the term *new media* Hemenway thinks about how changes in the technology of the book have shaped the way religious texts are written, collected, and read. How did the development of the codex contribute to the need to set a fixed canon of the Bible? How are new technologies for gathering and searching sacred texts producing new ways of engaging these writings?

References

Bhahba, Homi K. (1994) *The Location of Culture*, London: Routledge.

Campbell, Heidi A. (2010) *When Religion Meets New Media*, Abingdon: Routledge.

Campbell, Heidi A. (2012) "Understanding the Relationship between Religion Online and Offline in a Networked Society," *Journal of the American Academy of Religion*, Vol. 80, No. 1, March.

Clark, Lynn Schofield (2012) *The Parent App*, Oxford: Oxford University Press.

Hoover, Stewart and Echchaibi, Nabil (2012) *The "Third Spaces" of Digital Religion*, http://cmrc.colorado.edu/wp-content/uploads/2012/06/Hoover-Echchaibi-paper.pdf, Boulder, CO: The Center for Media, Religion, and Culture.

Manovitch, Lev (2001) *The Language of New Media*, Cambridge, MA: MIT Press.

Reflection
Gaming the end times

Rachel Wagner

El Shaddai: Ascension of the Metatron (UTV Ignition Entertainment, 2011) is a contemporary video game that explicitly draws on Judeo-Christian apocalyptic tradition. The game is based on legendary stories about Enoch, a character mentioned briefly in the book of Genesis in the Bible, who also has a very rich ancient apocryphal (extra-biblical) legacy of stories. In the ancient Jewish apocalypse and in later Jewish apocryphal mystical tradition, Enoch is depicted ascending through various levels or heavens, on a quest to understand the cosmos, guided by an angelic interpreter. Along the way, he is shown cosmological wonders, like where snow and hail are made, as well as visions of future judgment of the wicked and rewards for the righteous. *El Shaddai: Ascension of the Metatron* similarly relies upon the story of Enoch's ascension through levels of achievement, revealing a marked structural similarity between ancient apocalypses and contemporary video games. In both the ancient apocalypse and the video game, Enoch must confront various malicious adversaries who would hinder him in his goal of ascent. Indeed, the similarity between apocalyptic literature of antiquity and many modes of contemporary video game play is striking, since both are rooted in a fundamental distinction between "good" guys and "bad" guys, and both rely upon an eschatological worldview, that is, on the notion that an "end" is approaching, and a savior figure is needed to intervene on behalf of other human beings.

Both the ancient apocalypse and the game, remarkably, fit the definition of apocalypse developed by a team of biblical scholars in 1979, where they proposed that an "apocalypse" is:

> a genre of revelatory literature with a narrative framework, in which a revelation is mediated by an otherworldly being to a human recipient, disclosing a transcendent reality which is both temporal, insofar as it envisages eschatological salvation, and spatial insofar as it involves another, supernatural world.[1]

These scholars had in mind a whole set of ancient texts that were very popular around the turn of the first millennium among Jews and Christians. If we think about it, many other contemporary video games also exhibit elements of this definition, even if they don't directly draw on specific biblical books like *El Shaddai* does. Video games "reveal" other worlds to us; they also frequently include an otherworldly "guide" of some sort (think of Cortana in *Halo*, for example); and they certainly often involve violent battles against brazen enemies.

However, there is a key difference between ancient apocalypse and contemporary new media apocalypses. In ancient Jewish and Christian apocalypses, the savior figure is typically guided by a divine hand, taking the form of a powerful prophet or, in the case of Christianity, a messiah. In contrast, in contemporary video games the savior figure is instead *the player*, who often wields a weapon and defeats enemies through self-initiated and strongly encouraged violence. Today's video game apocalypses, then, are markedly more individually determinative and less dependent on the notion of an external deity for change in the world. In other words, today's violent video games suggest that, instead of counting on otherworldly intervention to right perceived wrongs, the individual human being must depend upon his or her own savvy and willingness to directly exercise violence toward a particular end. He or she must also be quick, careful, ruthless, and precise, in effect "playing God" themselves. Are these positive shifts or problematic ones in the way we view religious intervention in today's world? Does it matter that the ancient apocalypses were about real enemies (the oppressive Romans in ancient Israel) versus today's imagined ones (monsters, war opponents, aliens, etc.)? Which is more violent, the ancient text-based apocalypses or today's video game apocalypses? What do you think?

Note

1 The Society of Biblical Literature's (SBL) "Apocalypse Group", in J.J. Collins, *Semeia*, 14 [1979]: 9.

Reflection
Codex to Kindle

Michael Hemenway

Books have long provided a medium for the material expression of religion. The particular technologies of "book" used by different religious groups in different times shaped the way they articulate their religious identities and practices. Buddhist Sutras were written on palm leaf book technology and Jewish Torah is traditionally inscribed on scroll book technology, both existing long before the codex that we know today.

The codex, the bound volume with covers and a spine holding together multiple pages of text, rows of which line the shelves of libraries today, was a new media form in antiquity. By binding multiple sheets of papyrus or parchment together at a spine and folding the pages in half this new mediation of book offered advantages in accessing texts. Instead of rolling continuously through a text to find a particular location, as with a scroll, the codex provided non-linear access to the text. Readers could enter at any point and easily jump around in the text. How might this change in the form of religious books impact the way people imagined these texts or used these books in religious practice?

The codex enhanced the collection capabilities of the book. While technologies like the scroll were used for collections of texts, for example the Torah scroll containing five writings, the non-linear access facilitated by the codex technology changes the relationship of these collected texts. By the fourth century single codices contained large portions of what is now the Christian Bible. Collecting writings that once existed on separate scrolls into a single codex allowed non-linear access to any part of the collection. It mattered less where each item in a collection was located within the book. For example, in a Torah scroll, one must roll through Genesis to get to Exodus, while, in a codex, a reader simply opens the book 20 percent into the text. This may not sound like a meaningful distinction, but imagine for a minute, "How much of the way we conceptualize the world comes from the way we read?"

Ironically, as the codex increased the possibilities for collection and access, it loosened the ties between these related texts because each could be accessed on its own with relatively little awareness of what came before and after it. The non-linear access facilitated by the codex had the potential to atomize a text or a collection of texts by allowing the reader to jump into and out of the text at any point.

The clear beginning and end of a codex, emphatically represented by covers, heightened questions about what got included. The potential of a book to gather a collection between two covers expanded the politics of inclusion and exclusion. When the norm is to have several scroll books or several palm leaf books in a collection there is less pressure to decide what is included and what is excluded because people could easily add or discard texts. Binding the collection set a lasting determination of what was included. Do you think the Christians' desire to set a canon, to decide which religious texts would be included in their Bible, might have been shaped by their decision to collect their sacred texts in codex form (Figure 4.2)?

Today, e-books are again transforming the way we read and write religious texts. Some of these innovations have an analog in our ancient example of the codex. Though most e-books offer up anachronistic page turning and even digital library shelves for collecting books, search functions and libraries in the cloud exponentially expand on the non-linear access and collection capabilities of the codex. We can search for a single word in a book or in multiple books and move right to that spot in each text without "opening" the books and with little awareness that the passage searched is located in a particular part of a larger text. When bits of text become atomized the boundaries between books becomes fuzzy.

Imagine reading a book in Kindle reader on an iPad. The screen shows the cover of the book and lets you digitally turn the pages as you read. Yet, using the search functionality in Kindle reader, without even opening the book, you can search for "religion and media" and Kindle will take you to the first occurrence of that phrase in the book without your needing to understand that passage in relation to the whole of the book. The search index feature then jumps to the next occurrence of this phrase, again without you knowing anything about the larger landscape of the book. This is a radical non-linear access that is now being applied across digital collections as in Google Books. How might this change the way people read their religious books?

Figure 4.2 Bible and tablet computer

5 Stability and change

Key ideas

- Organized religions change over time and today contest with secularity to shape societies.
- Forms of communication and mediation are constantly changing. Adapting to media change alters the forms of religious practice and influences which doctrines, theological themes, and understandings are emphasized.
- Religion is inseparable from the forms of its mediation. As media culture changes, religious institutions and practices change.

In part because religious traditions seek to connect believers to something that transcends and interprets culture, religious communities often understand their practice and ideas to be static, an unchanging source of continuity over time. Some academic observers also treat religion as a static and unmediated activity whose social purpose is to conserve traditional values. Yet the historical study of lived religious traditions demonstrates that religion is fluid, changing over time and in different cultural contexts, sometimes conserving and at other times challenging cultural norms.

To understand religious traditions, it is necessary both to think about what has endured over time and to recognize the ways traditions have adapted to new cultures, issues, and contexts. For example, though Christians have a sense of fidelity to a 2,000-year tradition, Christianity looks quite different in different cultures and time periods. The beliefs and practices among Middle Eastern Christians in the first century, medieval European Catholics, and contemporary African Pentecostals are best understood when we give attention to their differences as well as their similarities. Religion adapts to changes in political and social structures, in style and taste, and in who holds power in society to produce new forms of religion, which are expressed in changes in religion's mediations.

Changes that make media technologies cheaper and simpler to use grant greater access to a wider number of people. When people from outside the traditional centers of religious authority take advantage of this access in order to experiment with new forms of practice and to reflect on their religious lives it creates new centers of power. This shift is typically met by resistance from established leaders and institutions whose power is confirmed by already established forms of media. Other chapters focus on the rise of new religious movements and consider how, in seemingly secular societies, other forms of cultural mediation such as nationalism or fandom may do the work of religion. This chapter explores how the changes in media and mediation have contributed to changes within traditional forms of religion.

The changing religious world

The concept of *religion* is a construction or category through which we try to understand a diverse range of beliefs and practices that we assume are related in some way. On the ground, religion is not an abstraction. People do not practice religion in general, they practice Judaism, Islam, Zoroastrianism, Candomblé, New Age, yoga, or some personal set of practice and belief which outsiders see as one expression of what they abstractly call religion. Understanding *religion* requires attention to the way particular religious traditions develop over time, how they are mediated in culture, and how traditions change as they respond to cultural change and adopt new forms of mediation.

The reader may have a personal spiritual practice or ascribe to no religion. Readers in Great Britain, Europe, Japan, Canada, or any number of regions of the United States, may have seen firsthand the decline of once-dominant religious traditions. Readers in other regions of the United States, or in Africa, or South America may have seen the rise of traditions that are new to these regions. A full picture of religion in the world requires that individuals and cultures be cautious about universalizing their own experience. The decline of some traditional forms of Christianity, the rise of Islam, the spread of Pentecostal Christianity, the secularization of Japan, or the growth of Buddhism in the West, must be put in wider context.

Some places, northern Europe being a striking example, have seen considerable decline in organized religion in the last half-century. The Nordic countries have been at the forefront of the move to establish clearly secular societies. In secular society one may believe or not. Secularity need not mean that there is no religion. Rather, the secular culture treats religion as a personal matter that has no place in the public square. This can be seen in efforts in some countries to ban the wearing of religious garb or overtly religious symbols in schools and other public settings.

Sweden, which had a long history of supporting a state church, disestablished the Church of Sweden in 2000. One Swedish researcher at Uppsala University, who is also a Lutheran pastor, suggests that, while Swedes report that they want the church to continue, they seldom attend. She suggests that today the church is a symbol of cultural identity that is important to many Swedes but which is largely disconnected from their actual practice (Marta Axner, personal communication). Though not as dramatic, the number of people who attend

Figure 5.1 Church for sale

worship services or proclaim membership in the churches and synagogues has dropped across much of the rest of Western Europe (Figure 5.1).

Many sociologists, most notably Peter Berger, once thought that secularization would privatize religion, eradicating it from public life, and that religion would become less plausible to individuals, leading them to lose faith, so that religion would largely die away. This idea has largely been rejected. Secularization is a significant process, yet institutional and emerging forms of religion continue. However, some scholars argue that the declines in religious affiliation that sociologists measure mark the passing of "Christendom," signaling the end of the conviction that there is a transnational society organized around Christian institutions and worldview (McLeod and Ustorf 2003).

Northern Europe is a helpful illustration of the interactions of religion and the secular. For all the evidence of secularization, religion has not disappeared from northern Europe or become only a matter of cultural heritage. Societies are complex, and this apparent turn from religion has not been absolute. The desire in some countries to ban religious clothing and other symbols from civic institutions like schools, the courts, and government offices has produced repeated conflicts among those who see the wearing of the Muslim headscarf in public as a vital expression of modesty, or a beard and turban as inherent to Sikh religious identity, and those who see these practices as an imposition of the religious into public space presumed to be inherently secular. In part, this is a matter of immigration; the trend toward secularization is challenged by the presence of migrants from the southern hemisphere. But even in the most secular of states it is not only immigrants who practice religion. Islam and other religions of the world have attracted converts in Europe. People also continue various forms of Christian and Jewish practice, return to pre-Christian practices, or adopt new religions.

Religious practice in the United States and Canada, particularly in some regions, is far more common than in northern Europe; however, even North America reports an overall continued decline in church membership and attendance (National Council of Churches 2010). Will the US and Canada continue to follow Europe toward more secular practice? Will religion become increasingly privatized, moving perhaps out of the physical and digital public square? As this volume goes to press, people in Quebec are debating "The Quebec Charter of Values" which, if passed, would ban the wearing of religious dress and symbols, at least by employees in schools, the courts, and other civic centers.

In the face of these changes it is understandable that some people ask whether the focus on individual religious identity combined with the decline in involvement in institutional forms of religion signifies the end of organized religion in Western societies. Certainly once-dominant religious groups have declined in influence, replaced both by a drop in overall affiliation and a more complex range of religious traditions and voices. Thus, news reports and scholarly studies are increasingly likely to focus on new and emerging religious movements and practices.

Secularity is a powerful movement, particularly in the northern hemisphere, and understanding this change is vital to understanding the history of religion in many regions. However, secularity and the privatization of religion are not the whole picture; the survey cited above that reports a gradual decline in church membership in North America also reports that almost 146 million people belong to churches in the US and Canada. An accurate description of the northern hemisphere must recognize the continued development of religious life in the face of the rise of secularity and the questions that these developments raise about religion.

Understanding the religious environment also requires attention to shifts in power and presence between religious institutions and movements themselves. In the United States there has been a decline in the non-Evangelical Protestant denominations that were once described as the religious mainline and thought to be able to speak for the nation on ethical issues. At the same time there has been growth in Evangelical and charismatic Christianity, Eastern religions, Islam, and new religious movements. In contrast to Europe, religious practice in North America is more common and often more evident in the public square. Since the European conquest of North America, Protestant Christianity has been the dominant form of religion on the continent, its hegemony sometimes creating a discourse of the United States as a "Christian nation." Increasingly Americans have come to recognize the diversity of their religious heritage. America was not lacking in religious practices when the first Europeans arrived. The First Nations of the North American continent have their own diverse indigenous religious traditions. European immigrants included free thinkers and Jews, Catholics, and Orthodox Christians as well as various types of Protestants. Asian immigrants brought animist, Buddhist, Taoist, Shinto, and Confucian practices. The forced migration of slaves brought both Islam and the indigenous religious practices of Africa to the Americas.

Any picture of the range of religions and their influence in societies around the world must be complex. The patterns of practice and change are uneven. Some places have far more obvious religious practice than others. It remains the case that around the world huge numbers of people identify with religious communities and institutions. The study of media, religion, and culture, then, must include an examination of how these religious groups respond to media change in different times and spaces.

The possibilities and limitations of media

If religion is inseparable from its mediation so that there is no unmediated religion against which we can measure contemporary practice, then religion exists in symbiotic relationship to the media through which it is expressed.

Thinking fairly conventionally about media, as though it were only a tool to illustrate something, we note that different tools have different effects. It follows that using different forms of media to express a religion will reveal different aspects of the tradition. The experience of listening to the Bach B Minor Mass, looking at Michelangelo's painting on the ceiling of the Sistine Chapel, or participating in a sacred dance on Easter morning are all artistic mediations of Christianity that evoke different bodily responses and draw attention to different elements of the religion (Figure 5.2). A new or different medium provides a fresh perspective and influences the way we think about religion.

This idea, that the available media influence how people practice religion, focuses attention on the relationship between media and religion. Thinking in this way treats religion and media as though they were separate things, one of

Figure 5.2 Sistine Chapel ceiling

which (media) expresses the other (religion). Religion and media are not so easily separated. Music, painting, writing, architecture, dance, and the new media of our day are not simply illustrations of religion; they are locations of religion itself. To stay with but one of the examples above, the vast space of the Sistine Chapel with its intricately painted ceiling is not merely an illustration of religion, it *is* religion at work, evoking in the Christian the vast and lasting power of their God, and of the empire organized in God's name. It is not enough to say that, when media change, our *perspective* on religion changes. If media and religion are intertwined in the way this book claims, then religion itself takes new form in the midst of media change.

The media/religion process can sound mechanistic, as if media technologies have an inevitable shaping effect on religion apart from what people do with them. That is also overly simplistic. Human agency is involved in the way that media are used. While technologies lend themselves to some possibilities and make others harder to envision, attention must be given to the human practices that develop around particular media tools.

Imagine you are watching a particularly beautiful sunset and pondering ways to convey the experience to your friends. You might mediate your experience in any of a number of ways. Perhaps you might address the phenomenon in purely scientific terms and write an essay analyzing how light refracted through pollution in the air produces a particular visual effect. Or, responding artistically, you might try to reproduce these patterns of light and color in a painting or capture them in a photograph. Perhaps the sunset evokes a sense of the sacred in you, a connection to something greater than yourself that transcends the everyday. If so, you might try to elicit a similar response from someone else. You might sing a song or tweet about your own emotional and religious responses to the sight. You could write a theological treatise arguing that nature reveals a creator. In each case, the medium you choose lends itself to suggesting part, but not all, of your original experience. Even a multi-media presentation that combined all these mediations of your experience of the sunset would not be the experience itself. Further, your original experience of viewing the sunset is itself shaped by mediation. If you grew up hearing John Denver sing *Sunshine on My Shoulders*, or are familiar with Thomas Kincade's use of glowing light in his idealistic paintings of American scenes, these things become lenses through which you view the sunset. If, on the other hand, your imagination is shaped by films and literature that use light and explosions as an apocalyptic image of a frightening end history, you might see the sunset differently.

Religious practitioners experience the sacred, and communicate their beliefs and practices, through some form of mediation. Whether they use sacred texts, theological arguments, rituals, spaces, images, scents, or sounds the medium they choose encourages particular ways of thought and practice. Reflecting on this, a University of Chicago blogger suggests, "We must confront the reality that a medium by the very terms of its existence remediates. It absorbs the form and content of other media and reworks, reconfigures, or otherwise refashions them" (Chakravorty 2012).

In illustration of the complex relationship between a mediation and the thing it signifies, the surrealist artist René Magritte (1898–1967) famously painted a work titled "The Treachery of Images." It is a picture of a tobacco pipe above the words *Ceci n'est pas une pipe* ("This is not a pipe"). With this cryptic caption the artist reminds us that what we see is paint and canvas, an image of *une pipe*, not the pipe itself. Yet a rich portrayal elicits something in the human response that connects powerfully to the objects and experiences portrayed. In this case the painting evokes the idea of a pipe and perhaps reminds us of a famous pipe smoker like Sherlock Holmes or more complexly the smells and emotions connected to a family member who smokes a pipe. Similarly, one might look at a statue of the Buddha and easily recognize that it is a statue, not the Buddha. Still, the statue calls to mind the historical figure and his legacy. More than that, the mediation of the central figure of Buddhism evokes the beliefs and practices which are associated with the religion. For the practitioner of Buddhism such mediations are an inseparable part of the religion itself.

Resistance and adaptation to media change

Some religious traditions are concerned that the complexity of the relationship between the signification and the signified leads to idolatry. Magritte is hinting at this phenomenon with his pipe painting: The painting is not a pipe, just as a statue of the Buddha is not the Buddha. Traditions more open to image think people understand that the statue invites the practitioner's reflection on the Buddha. Other traditions have feared that this distinction is not so easily made and fear that such images would be revered instead of the sacred thing being represented by the statue, painting, or other image.

Expressing this concern, the Hebrew Scriptures speak of Yahweh as one who, unlike the deities of the Israelites' neighbors, cannot be portrayed. In the story of the golden calf, Moses becomes angry when he sees the Israelites turning to the golden statue portraying the Canaanite deity Ba'al and he smashes the stone tablets containing the Ten Commandments. During the Reformation in Europe, early Protestants destroyed religious paintings and smashed stained glass windows to express their desire for a pure and unmediated experience of God.

This rejection of images did not mean that these traditions did not have their own esthetic or produce their own sacred spaces that mediated their understanding of the sacred (Goethals 1990). These early Protestants and the Israelites before them wanted to ensure that the images themselves were not becoming a focus of adoration, and they wanted to create conditions so that believers could have what they imagined would be a pure, unmediated religious experience.

Sunni Muslims, historically, have also taken this approach toward representational images of their sacred figures. They find attempts to depict the Prophet Muhammad particularly offensive. Again, this does not mean that their traditional religion does not have its own mediations; think, for example, of the esthetic expressed in the architecture of a traditional mosque or in the elegant calligraphy that often illuminates verses of the Qur'an. Sunnis believe that the beautiful can point to the divine, but they also fear that when an image of the divine is too concrete it can be confused with that to which it is pointing.

For Jews, Christians, and Muslims the ambivalence about image expresses a theological concern that nothing come between the people and the Holy One. However real that concern, this book argues that we have no experience of the divine that is not embedded in the human mediations of that experience.

Much of the popular discourse about religion and media expresses a similar concern that mediation dilutes some pure experience of religion. This may be due more to anxiety about change than to a concern about how people actually practice religion. Books like Allan Bloom's *The Closing of the American Mind* (1987) seem to treat religion as though it were a fixed reality that is now beset by acculturated media change. In this view, mediations are seen as debasing religion. However, the relationship between media and religion is unavoidable. There was no pre-media golden age of religion. Media/religion/culture is and always has been historically located and is thus a changing phenomenon.

Though change often produces anxiety, societies seldom reject new forms of media. Even Amish Christians with their horse-drawn buggies and traditional dress do not reject change outright. It is a misunderstanding of the nature of their religious lives to conclude that the Amish simply choose to live in the past. Rather, they are slow adopters, carefully evaluating the impact of new technologies on their family and community life. For instance, many Amish opt not to have a telephone in their homes, but they may allow it in the workplace for reasons of commerce and safety. Phone booths are sometimes positioned at the intersection of farms so that several families can share them for approved purposes without the phones disrupting the household (Umble 1992).

Media scholar Heidi Campbell studies the ways in which religious communities both resist and adapt to new media. She calls this social adaptation of technology to religious purposes the "middle way." Among the groups she studies are ultra-Orthodox Jewish communities in Israel who have worked out religiously acceptable ways to control access to the Internet. In ways similar to how the Amish adapted to the telephone, the ultra-Orthodox Jews considered whether the Internet would disrupt community life and introduce religiously inappropriate outside influences. They weighed this concern against the possibility that the Internet could be a useful tool for Jewish education and commerce. As a result, they developed kosher tools that could screen out objectionable material and steer users toward approved sites and sources (Campbell 2010).

Both those who adapt to media change and those who resist new media cultures are impacted by media change. Media change contributes to changes in religious practice, alters centers of authority, and shifts theological emphasis. In Chapter 6 we will consider, for instance, how Evangelical broadcasters adopted the mode of the television talk show, including its valorization of celebrity culture, and how this media practice changed Evangelical religious practice. One small piece of evidence that Christian communities are seeking to adapt to new media technologies can be seen when clergy who once resisted the use of television have installed big screens in their sanctuaries so they can provide graphic illustration of their sermons or simply make it easier for a large congregation to see what is going on. Preachers also adapt to the parameters of the medium of television and the norms of communication that it establishes even when they are not using video images in worship. Because TV and other forms of media have contributed to people's shorter attention spans, ministers preach shorter sermons and lead worship services that have more visually and aurally stimulating activity. Both thoughtful students of religion and media and self-aware religious practitioners endeavor to understand how both resistance to and adoption of emerging media contribute to changes in the practices, theologies, doctrines, and locations of religions.

Changing locations of authority

Religious institutions and traditions turn to multiple forms of authority, including religious texts, councils, and authority figures such as the Dalai Lama or the Pope that establish and interpret right doctrine and practice. In times of change, when believers experience conflict between these and other cultural centers of authority, the power of these individuals, religious texts, and councils, is often questioned, and new unofficial "authorities" can emerge.

Today social media create a space for these alternative voices. New authorities emerge who may lack traditional credentials but who have command of the new medium. For instance in Islam, particularly in the Shi'a tradition, Imams are trained in particular historic traditions and their authority rests on a combination of charisma within the community, training, and location within these traditions. But new media have given voice to a variety of online, radio, or television teachers of Islam from outside those traditions, and often trained in secular universities. They challenge the traditional authorities, opening a wider debate about Islamic life today (Echchaibi 2012).

The use of new forms of media as a location for religious innovation is not a new phenomenon; new or appropriated media have always provided means for lay and folk movements to develop new symbols and practices that contend with religious authorities' efforts to shape practice and doctrine. In medieval times the carnival provided a relatively safe space to mock the priests and lords of the manor, as have its popular culture descendants such as film, television, and comics. The practice of venerating Our Lady of Guadalupe (one of the cultural manifestations of Mary the mother of Jesus), which first emerged among the poor in Mexico in the sixteenth century, has myriad contemporary expressions in folk art, tattoos, pilgrimages, and home altars. Something similar is happening when common people in East Asia incorporate the images and actions of animistic practice into folk Buddhism. Paying attention to these mediations of alternative spiritualities and practices reminds us that religion goes where it will. New practices and voices emerge to meet unmet needs, in so doing empowering new centers of religious life.

A concrete example of how media, religion, and culture change in relationship to each other can be found in Isabel Hofmeyr's study of how John Bunyan's allegorical Protestant novel *The Pilgrim's Progress* was transformed as it was taken out of its original European context and put into a vastly different one. The seventeenth-century English novel was hugely popular among European Protestants. Missionaries carried the book with them to Africa, where over time it was translated into some 80 African languages. In the process of translation into new languages and cultures, various concepts within the book took on different meanings. Bunyan's focus on original sin was of central importance to his European readers. Original sin, as an explanation of the fall of humankind, was not, however, a crucial doctrine for African Christians. As a result, the images in the novel were interpreted differently by African translators and readers. The idea of original sin drops out of the African translations, or it takes new meanings. Hofmeyr writes, "The most famous image of Bunyan's story, namely the burden on Christian's [the protagonist's] back, stood for original sin. In many African editions, this meaning is erased, and instead the burden comes to stand for colonial rule itself" (Hofmeyr in Morgan 2008: 206). Hofmeyr's account of these translations reveals the complex interaction of media, religion, and culture. When missionaries bring European Christianity to Africa, both the religion and the receiving culture are changed by their interaction. The translations of *The Pilgrim's Progress* were a location of an emerging African Christianity with a distinctive theology appropriate to the needs and worldview of Africans.

Noticing changes in the water

The speed of media change in contemporary societies makes us aware of how religion and media are linked in ways that were less evident in periods when change was slower. Some observers see the way religion is changing in our fast-paced digital culture as a positive development leading to new and more relevant forms of religious life. Others believe that some earlier essence of religion is being lost or trivialized in these interactions. Whatever judgment people make about the way religion is changing today, it is necessary to recognize that this is not a new phenomenon; religion has always embedded new media technologies and it changes in response to new possibilities of expression.

Chapter 1 made the analogy that people live in media cultures like fish live in water, suggesting that it is hard to recognize the pervasive influence of media. That analogy rests on the assumption that the media culture in which we "swim" is relatively stable and therefore goes unnoticed. When media change comes slowly, we hardly recognize how these technologies of communication affect religion. But when radical changes in communications systems occur and media change accelerates, as is happening at present, our attention is drawn to the intersections of religion and media and the way both are transformed as a result. When the water changes, the fish ask, "What is changing and what impact will it have on us?"

Writing and print technologies serve as historical examples of how once new media technologies that had a profound effect on religion are now so established that we largely ignore their influence. Many, though not all, religions possess writings that their adherents regard as sacred. Examples include the Qur'an, the Bhagavad Gita, the Book of Mormon, the Torah, the Upanishads, and the Bible. It is long established that people use the written word to capture religious histories, stories, legal codes, and teachings, and that practitioners study, reflect on, and venerate these sacred writings. It seems unremarkable to us that people preserve their histories, sacred stories, and rules in this way. Yet we know that preliterate cultures had religions that did not rely on sacred texts; their sense of the sacred was orally communicated in stories, expressed in rituals, and preserved in sacred objects or spaces, all passed down through the generations. Once we see that religion is possible without sacred texts, a whole series of questions emerge. How did religion change when writing and literacy made such texts possible? What were these religions or their predecessors like before their sacred texts were written, gathered, and interpreted? How did the adherents decide which writings were uniquely inspired? Which voices were privileged and which suppressed in that process? Did they adopt or resist later media change such as the printing press, audio and visual recording, or the Internet?

In preliterate religion there was a unique power in knowing and being able to recount in a compelling manner the oral histories and sacred stories of one's community. The storyteller's ability provided the authority to guide the community in the present. Writing shifted that power base. The literate, with their power to capture and rework those stories, creating a written record, came to power. They shaped the new practices that emerged around reading, interpreting, and venerating the sacred writings.

Remembering how religion interacted with the rise of literacy and writing should remind those who study the relationship between religion and media today that this is not a new relationship. People's questions about the rise of digital communication are similar to the challenge raised by the rise of literacy. As digital media take on some of the roles once filled by earlier forms of mediation, those who participate in these new forms of communication will inevitably shape new expressions of religion. The digital realm provides a forum for discussion and a location for the expression of human feelings. People will create new digital spaces that contest with the old physical architecture of the sacred. What has changed in our era is not that religion is embedded in media culture for the first time but that media change is taking place so quickly that we are more likely to notice it.

Discussion questions

1 The chapter suggests that religions change over time, and that their place and function in society changes. Paradoxically, today many societies see both greater religious diversity and a rise in the secular. What evidence of these changes do you see in your local and national community? How do these changes alter the way people think about religion and its role in society?

2 Some people suggest that media are so powerful that the internal logic of new forms of media imposes changes on religion. Others suggest that it is more important to pay attention to how people adopt and adapt these new forms. Which argument seems more compelling, and what evidence do you see for your answer?

3 As illustrated by the Magritte painting titled "The Treachery of Images," the relationship between an esthetic image and the object or person it evokes is complex. This is perhaps even more complicated when the visual reference is to the sacred. How do images evoke the sacred, and what anxieties does the religious use of images evoke? What makes an object, image, or place sacred? Is there some experience of the sacred, holy, or numinous apart from the way they are mediated? If so, what is it?

4 If visual media can evoke the sacred, can they also be blasphemous? Is this a matter of the content of the image, or of the way people use the image? Does the text of a Buddhist incantation mean something different, or perform different religious and cultural work, when it appears as a tattoo on the body of celebrity actress Angelina Jolie rather than on the wall of a Buddhist temple in Bangkok? Does an image of Our Lady of Guadalupe serve different purposes or have different meanings on the wall of a chapel in rural Mexico, in a home altar in a barrio of Los Angeles, or on a tee shirt worn by an Agnostic Anglo hipster?

5 The chapter discusses the way that African Christians appropriated *The Pilgrim's Progress*. How and why did they interpret the novel differently than the European missionaries who brought it to the continent? What do we learn about how art and literature have meaning, and about the relationships between media, religion, and culture, from reflecting on this example?

6 The following reflections both deal with the way religious communities have adopted emerging forms of media. Echchaibi reflects on an alternative Muslim website intended to serve Muslims in the West, and Morgan on an image that illustrates the way eighteenth-century Protestants adapted to the emergence of inexpensive print technologies. How do the two communities use these new forms of media? Who is the audience for these new forms of religious media? Who is given voice through them, and does this cause a shift in who holds religious authority? If we think of eighteenth-century tracts and images and twenty-first-century websites as places where religious identity is being performed, what do we learn about the producers and consumers of these images and messages?

References

Berger, Peter L. (1967) *The Sacred Canopy: Elements of a Sociological Theory of Religion*, Garden City: Doubleday.

Bloom, Allan (1987) *The Closing of the American Mind*, New York: Simon & Schuster.

Campbell, Heidi (2010) *When Religion Meets New Media*, Abingdon: Routledge.

Campbell, Heidi, ed. (2012) *Digital Religion: Understanding Religious Practice in New Media Worlds*, London: Routledge.

Chakravorty, Swagato (2012) "Mediation." (blog) Chicago School of Media Theory, http://lucian.uchicago.edu/blogs/mediatheory/keywords/mediation, accessed November 5, 2012.

Echchaibi, Nabil (2012) "Alt-Muslim: Muslims and Modernity's Discontents," in Heidi Campbell, ed. *Digital Religion: Understanding Religious Practice in New Media Worlds*, London: Routledge.

Goethals, Gregor T. (1990) *Electronic Golden Calf*, Cambridge: Cowley Publications.

Hofmeyr, Isabel (2004) *The Portable Bunyan: A Transnational History of The Pilgrim's Progress*, Princeton, NJ: Princeton University Press.

McLeod, Hugh and Werner Ustorf, eds. (2003) *The Decline of Christendom in Western Europe, 1750–2000*, Cambridge: Cambridge University Press.

Morgan, David, ed. (2008) *Keywords in Religion, Media and Culture*, London: Routledge.

National Council of Churches (2010) *Yearbook of American and Canadian Churches*, New York: National Council of Churches.

Umble, Diane Zimmerman (1992) "The Amish and the Telephone: Resistance and Reconstruction," *Consuming Technologies: Media and Information in Domestic Spaces*, London: Routledge.

Reflection

Altmuslim

Media spaces for a modern Muslim voice

Nabil Echchaibi

Who can speak on behalf of Islam and who is a Muslim? Islam has no official authority figure or central clerical structure that represent the faith. A rather pluralistic and diffuse notion of authority has always defined this religion. Historically, Muslims have vested some of that authority in a variety of religious scholars and charismatic leaders of Sunni, Shi'a, and Sufi Islam. Such a decentralization has been recently intensified by rising literacy rates and wider access to media technologies in Muslim majority countries as well as by an increasing presence of Muslims in secular Western countries.

Shortly after the tragic events of 9/11, an American Muslim of Pakistani descent launched *Altmuslim.com* as an introspective space for Muslims to offer critical perspectives on Muslim life, politics, and culture. With contributing editors and writers from the United States, Canada, Australia, and the UK, *Altmuslim* positions itself at the forefront of an emerging independent Muslim media in the West. Its articles, opinions, media reviews, podcasts, and video commentaries seek to project an alternative view of Muslims as intellectuals, politicians, and artists. Postings from contributors with a wide range of ideological orientations and religious sensibilities have included commentaries on the "Gay Muslim Phenomenon," Muslim views on divorce, female Muslim artists, social justice in Islam, and Muslim American graffiti. Shahed Amanullah, the founder of *Alt-Muslim*, does not think of himself as a religious authority, but his site has over the years promoted a dynamic conversation about Islam by non-traditional and heretofore excluded Muslim voices (Figure 5.3). Through a careful grooming of new Muslim commentators, *Altmuslim* seeks to mediate a diverse religious experience and create an alternative frame of reference for self-definition for other Muslims. The site addresses Muslims as producers of their own knowledge about their faith and encourages them to imagine ways in which their religion can be harmonized with modernity.

In the wake of the national debate on gay marriage, for instance, *Altmuslim* published two different viewpoints on homosexuality in Islam: one favorable opinion by a feminist in Cincinnati, a member of Muslims

Figure 5.3 Website founder Shahed Amanullah

for Progressive Values, and the other an opposite view by a poet and activist in Brooklyn. Despite their wildly divergent views using two different readings of the Qur'anic narrative of Lot, both authors recognized the urgency to address what is largely a taboo topic in Muslim communities and invited their readers to engage in a reasoned debate about theological interpretations of homosexuality in Islam and the limits and virtues of their relevance in a secular and pluralistic democracy. By soliciting this kind of heated commentary, *Altmuslim* tries to jumpstart an important dialogue about sensitive issues that average Muslims are eager to discuss but don't have the opportunity or the platforms to share their opinions.

Another significant feature of *Altmuslim* is its creative appropriation of non-linear digital esthetics and interactive communication modes to draw Muslims into an alternative religious experience. Besides reading provocative commentaries, site visitors are invited to rate their mosque experience, read and leave reviews on *Zabihah*—a guide to local halal restaurants and products—and shop for Muslim apparel, toys, books, music, and more on *halalapalooza*, a site that Amanullah has designed to direct traffic to halal commercial companies. More than just a space for debate, *Altmuslim* has harnessed the power of digital media to project a model for an active Muslim subject and prescribe religious ways to intervene and domesticate modern public space and secular practices.

Reflection
Religious tracts in the eighteenth century

David Morgan

Speaking, reading, writing, and hearing were regarded by Anglo-American Protestants in the late eighteenth and early nineteenth century as the indispensable and authoritative means of transmitting and learning the Gospel. Reading was rapidly becoming the most important form of communication as print production and circulation expanded across the transatlantic British Empire. Newspapers, magazines, almanacs, tracts, and sermons were dominant print media during the period. The more people became used to reading, the more Evangelical organizations turned to print to reach them.

Organizations began to form during the 1790s in England and slightly later in America to produce and distribute pious print, focusing on children, immigrants, the poor, and laborers as well as prostitutes, drinkers, sailors, soldiers, infidels, gamblers, and theater-goers—all populations whom Evangelicals felt were at risk in the emerging industrial revolution, which conducted a massive migration of peoples from the countryside to urban life. The shift threatened traditional social arrangements. Religious tract, Sunday school, Bible, and Mission societies issued an astonishing variety of print products aimed at these groups in order to compete with the secular print that vied for their attention.

Although the spoken word was considered by many Protestants to be the foremost medium for publishing the Good News, print was the more practical means for broadcasting to an expanding world what Protestants believed was necessary to be "heard." But advocates of religious print refused to concede a contradiction. They argued that print fitted seamlessly over speech, and they encouraged authors to produce tracts written in common style, using speech and diction derived from spoken discourse. Leaders of publication societies in Britain and America wanted writing to be patterned on speaking, and they argued for the ancient continuity of speech and writing. One of the founders of the Religious Tract Society in Britain proclaimed that "God himself [was] the author of a short religious tract: with his own hands he wrote the Ten Commandments of the law."[1] The idea flattened the distinction between speaking and writing, hearing and reading, and launched Protestant evangelism in a global flurry of print.

When Evangelicals imagined the work of evangelism, they envisioned preaching as an ideal speech act: one that suffered no translation from one

Figure 5.4 The Christian Almanac

language and culture to another, and one in which the European or American preacher could hold forth in a direct articulation of the Bible as the recorded word of God. The illustration in Figure 5.4 captures this dream of universal direct discourse very well. The neatly dressed missionary orates with Bible in hand before a gathering of people from around the world. Asians, Native Americans, Africans, and Middle Easterners listen contentedly to the Anglo preacher whose speech Anglo-American missionary societies converted into scores of languages during the nineteenth century.

Note

1 David Bogue, *The Diffusion of Divine Truth* (London: printed by S. Rousseau for the Religious Tract Society, 1800): 11.

6   Organized religion in the age of digital media

Key ideas

- Organized religion reflects the internal logic and style of the media cultures within which it developed.
- Religion both adopts and resists media change.
- New media can provide locations for emerging religion.
- Religious practitioners are often unreflective about the implications of the media and thus unprepared for the way they reshape faith and practice.

The relationships between media, religion, and culture are mutual. Neither media, religion, nor culture is fixed; moreover, they are each changed through their interactions with one another. As we have seen in earlier chapters, this connection between media, religion, and culture is not a new development. Religion has always been mediated, and it is inseparable from the forms of its mediation. To say we are studying religion *and* media is only to make explicit our awareness of this inevitable connection. Our subject matter is rightly the entire history of religion in its multiple mediations.

Through religion people seek to relate to the ineffable, to something beyond culturally limited human experience. Yet humans cannot stand outside our own historical and cultural finitude to observe religion at work. We see religion as it is expressed in particular cultural mediations. This process is particularly evident when new forms of communication emerge, providing new locations for the religious imagination. Language, the capacity to make images and art, the development of systems of writing, the growth of literacy, and the emergence of technologies such as the printing press, radio, TV, and film did more than expand the range of messages. These forms of expression enabled new ways of being human and, through emerging forms of media, individuals and cultures found new ways to relate to and articulate that ineffable something beyond their experience.

Locating religion in the digital age

The most recent media revolution has been the digitalization of image and information, the emergence of the Internet, and the rise of various forms of social media. As with past media revolutions, various questions arise. What does religion look like in the midst of this monumental shift? How do individuals, movements, and institutions adapt to the new communications technologies that rapidly divide text and image into infinitely variable building blocks, create new "spaces" and relationships, and allow data to be sampled, edited, and reorganized with a click of the mouse? What sort of persons and societies are we becoming, and what forms of religious practice are emerging that speak of the ineffable sacred in these new media spaces? Where shall we look for vibrant examples of religion at work in digital culture?

Chapter 2 explored the way that contemporary religious practice has become individualized and focused on the self rather than on the life of organized religious communities. The chapter expounded on the idea that the contemporary religious project, at least for people in the United States and Europe, is one of individual identity construction (Hoover 2006). It looked at the ways that, in a period in which many describe themselves as "spiritual but not religious," individuals construct their religious identities, often by drawing on ideas and practices from multiple sources.

Religion scholar Sarah Pike suggests that religion is more fully understood when it is examined at the margins of society. Her interests are wide ranging. She studies the practices of groups ranging from Muslim punks to Neopagans. Pike reflects on the conflicts and accommodations that Hmong immigrants to the United States make to integrate both traditional shamanic practice and fundamentalist Christianity in their religious lives. Pike says that significant religious activity takes place in "other spaces" including "alternative religions on the internet, shrines and altars in unexpected places, backyard and roadside religion, and music subcultures and festivals" (Pike 2008: 171).

Chapter 4 introduced the notion that many contemporary people draw their identity from networks of relationships that loosely connect them to multiple communities rather than by participating in a single core community. This suggests that organized religions and local religious communities such as mosques, temples, synagogues, and churches may become less important as they become only one part of the religious or spiritual network within which people move.

The way that religion has become a matter of personal construction, performed at the margins of society or expressed in loose networks, draws our attention to significant emerging patterns of religious practice and belief. This phenomenon, however, can mask the continued presence and influence of organized and institutionalized religion. This chapter looks at how established religious communities respond to media change.

Organized religion in the digital age

The current status of organized religion in the world is more complex than a simple narrative of decline would suggest. It is true that in some parts of the world participation in organized religion has declined. But huge numbers of people worldwide still identify with some form of organized religion. The Pew

Research Center writes, "The world's Muslim population is expected to increase by about 35% in the next 20 years, rising from 1.6 billion in 2010 to 2.2 billion by 2030" (2011: 1). Hindus are generally recognized as the third largest religious community after Christians and Muslims and their numbers are thought to approach 1 billion people. In sections of Africa and in Latin America Pentecostal Christianity has seen huge growth. The picture in the northern hemisphere is mixed. Some regions have become more secular, but migration and other factors have also introduced new traditions in places where long-held religious practices have declined. The Nordic countries are an example of these changes: their populations are increasingly being described as secular, and once-dominant Christian practices have faded. Many immigrants to the region from Islamic cultures bring their religion with them, contesting this image of the secular state. A full picture of religion in the Nordic countries, and similar societies, requires attention to the rise of the secular and the resulting decline of particular traditions and practices. However, these changes must be considered in relationship to the way existing religions adapt and traditions new to the region emerge, and to the cultural tensions between these new tendencies. Many people in a range of countries still affiliate with organized religion, so the study of religion and media needs to consider how those religious communities and their institutions respond to media change.

Adaptations to media change in American Christianity

How do organized religious communities adapt to changing media environments? How are they shaped by their adoption of, or resistance to, new media? Religious organizations make use of media for internal communication, to speak to the wider society about a variety of moral and civil issues, and as a setting for ritual practice. Religious identity becomes tied to these forms of expression, leading established religious communities to sometimes resist communication changes, fearing that new ways of communication will distort their message and alter their practice. This was evident in the suspicion of many established Christian groups of the development of television. They thought the form too insubstantial and impersonal for primary religious communication and thus largely left television to emerging religious groups. A similar thing may be happening with social media.

As early as the 1980s, in discussing the tendency of established religious leaders to resist new forms of media, Bible and media scholar Tom Boomershine cited the biblical account of the early sixth-century BCE ruler of Judah, King Jehoiakim, as an example of resistance to the power of religious media. The prophet Jeremiah confronts the presumably divinely appointed King, by reading aloud from the new media of the day, a scroll, recounting the prophet's criticism of the king (Jeremiah 36:1–32). King Jehoiakim responds by burning the scroll and ordering the prophet's arrest. Boomershine claims that most mainline American Christians similarly resist new media when they challenge their way of doing things, suggesting that they want to live in the print communications world where American religious practices were first developed. He notes that religious communities that overcome this resistance and adapt successfully to media change increase their role in society, and cites the rise of British and American Methodism in the seventeenth century as due in part to their adaptation to the changes in print technologies that allowed the cheap printing and distribution of pamphlets and song books (lectures and personal communication). David Morgan's more recent work on religious tracts further develops this history (1999). Such ideas are moving increasingly into public discourse. A 2011 article in the weekly magazine *The Economist* was titled "Social Media in the 16th Century: How Luther Went Viral." The article's author argues that five centuries before new media played a role in organizing and advancing the democratic uprisings in many Muslim nations that came to be called the Arab Spring, Martin Luther's use of what could be called the "social media" of his day helped bring about the Protestant Reformation (Standage 2011).

Television and the consequence of adapting, or not adapting, to media change

Previous media changes, such as from oral to written communication, or the invention of the printing press and the resulting spread of literacy, did more than accelerate the spread of existing religious messages. They reorganized practice, allowing new relationships to emerge, and in the process people developed new understandings of their religious beliefs and practices. The same process of resistance and adaptation is going on as established religions adapt to a changing media culture today.

Under pressure to adapt to new forms of media, religious communities have typically taken one of two approaches. Some assume that media are merely containers into which an unchanged message can be inserted. Thus they adopt new forms of media but with little attention to how their own practices, understandings, and assumptions change in the process. Others recognize that media change will lead to changes in their practices and understandings and, in order to defend the purity of forms of religion tied to the last media revolution, or to the forms of media common when their tradition emerged, they resist media change and are slow adopters of new forms of mediation. It is less common for religious leaders or communities to embrace new media technologies *and* be reflective about how these changes may introduce new ways of relating, new religious practices, or alternative systems of religious authority.

The response of various groups of American Christians to the spread of television provides vibrant examples of these tendencies toward unreflective adaptation or resistance. Unlike nations like Great Britain, where television and radio were developed as public systems, in the United States they developed primarily as commercial enterprises. The airwaves themselves, however, were understood to be a public resource, and broadcasters were granted license to use them in ways that, at least in theory, served the interest of the viewing public. Although broadcasters interpreted "the public good" and the values of their communities in a variety of ways, norms arose that television broadcasters would cover the news and provide some form of public service programming. The Federal Communications Commission (FCC) established that religious programming was one appropriate form of public service broadcasting.

To meet their obligation for public service, commercial stations began to donate difficult-to-sell Sunday morning airtime for religious broadcasting. The programming was produced by already established and dominant religious groups who were assumed to articulate widely shared religious values. Typically they did this relatively inexpensively in production space made available by the networks or local stations at little or no cost. The National Council of Churches (a federation of the then "mainline" Protestant denominations), the Roman Catholic Church, and to a lesser extent liberal Jewish groups produced public affairs programming with a religious focus and children's programs, and broadcast worship services, thus effectively controlling this religious space. The assumption of these groups was that these programs were supplemental to face-to-face congregational worship. In fact, one Roman Catholic program was called "Mass for Shut-ins," signaling that it was suitable only for those who could not attend mass in the brick-and-mortar sanctuary of their local parish.

This established system of religious broadcasting began to be challenged in the 1960s. The FCC ruled that paid religious programming also met the obligation of stations to serve the needs of their communities. In the mid-1970s a process of deregulation began, expanded during the Reagan administration, which treated broadcasting more as a commercial enterprise than a public trust. Religious broadcasting itself became a commercial enterprise. The growth of cable television in the mid-1980s and '90s radically increased the number of outlets, making it increasingly practical for entrepreneurial religious groups to market their own programming or even create their own stations and networks.

As free public service opportunities died away in the face of deregulation, the primary response of the established religious groups to television outside their public service niche was one of suspicion. Confident of their place in society and suspicious that television could do the substantive work of religion, the established mainstream religious groups did not make the investments needed to continue broadcasting. Because they saw the media as something separate from religion and accepted the popular description of television as a "vast wasteland," they saw their role as one of ethical critique. Through the National Council of Churches, they tended to support the development of media standards and the regulation of what they understood to be television's excesses.

Of course, the impact of television on American religious practice was not only seen in the content of the programming. For good or ill a television-oriented society operated under the expectation that people should be stimulated and entertained. Television encouraged multi-tasking and shortened attention spans. Dominant religious groups largely saw efforts to adapt to these cultural changes as an unfaithful acquiescence to popular culture and, at least subconsciously, resisted such changes. This resistance can be understood partly in terms of social class. The dominant religious voices in the early television era were tied to the upper-middle class. They saw television as a lower-class activity, even if they watched it themselves. Their resistance also expressed a theological concern rooted in their recognition that media change, in conjunction with other forces, would lead to changes in religious practice, which in turn might lead to changes in belief.

Evangelicals, in contrast, were much more entrepreneurial. The emergence of Evangelical broadcasting outside the public service ghetto is evidence of Evangelicals' faster adaptation to media change. They seized the broadcasting opportunity created by a free market and this contributed to the growth of Evangelical Christianity in the United States and, as their programs were exported, the spread of Evangelicalism in the developing world. In the meantime, the anxiety felt by once-dominant religious groups toward media change played a role in the decline of mainline Protestant authority.

While the old mainline churches paid a price for failing to move into the new media culture, the readiness of Evangelicals to uncritically embrace television broadcasting was not without its costs. Inserting an unchanging religious message into a new form of mediation was not, it turned out, as easy as Evangelicals had assumed. With programs like Pat Robertson's "The 700 Club," Evangelicals embraced the talk-show format of the "Tonight Show," which was cheap to produce when compared with narrative television and allowed the host a clear voice of hierarchical authority (Figure 6.1). The makers of these shows seemed heedless, however, of the way that the values of the larger celebrity culture were embedded in the format they embraced. The hosts of such programs paraded a series of actors, musicians, politicians, and sports figures across the stage to legitimize Evangelical practice and belief. Preacher hosts like Robertson, Jimmy Swaggart, and Jim and Tammy Faye Bakker became celebrities in their own right and often adopted the excesses and entitlements of celebrity life as signs of divine blessing. The financial and sexual scandals of broadcasters like Swaggart and the Bakkers resulted in part from the unregulated celebrity culture that religious broadcasting created.

Figure 6.1 Pat Robertson on set

Evangelical culture in America both grew and changed as it embraced the forms of television. Worship became a spectator sport, something one watched more than one did. This was true not only on television but also in the mega-churches that shared in the embrace of media culture. Here also preachers became celebrity performers, and worshipers, audience members. In this process, Evangelicalism grew by becoming more like the surrounding culture. In order to reach more people they unreflectively surrendered their minority identity with its demand for distinctive Christian practice.

More could be said about this transition. But for the moment it is enough to say that mainline American Protestantism shrank in an era when it failed to adapt to new technology and to the new forms of practice it invited. Meanwhile, Evangelicalism grew, partially because of its uncritical adoption of new forms of media, but it changed in unforeseen ways because it failed to anticipate the implications of its media choices.

Challenges and possibilities in the digital age

Does the American church's experience in the age of television foreshadow the way in which religious groups will respond to the digital age? Again, today we see that established religious figures, institutions, and movements are challenged by the emergence of new media cultures. What at first appear to be merely new ways of communicating are in fact locations where new forms of society arise. What will religion look like in digital culture, what new forms of religion will develop, and how will established religions adapt to this changing context? Which religions, religious communities, and religious leaders will cling to the belief that a pure essence of their religion is fixed and embedded in past forms of mediation, thus resisting new media's forms and the social assumptions and practices that grow up around it? Who will critically and creatively establish religion in these new social spaces?

It seems that some religious leaders are again making the mistake of assuming that new media are just containers. Or they think that media are simply amplifiers that allow them to be better heard in the midst of a wider media buzz. They try to duplicate face-to-face practices and express their current theologies and social agendas through new media. In doing so, they are likely to miss the way that today's new media reflect changing models of authority. Formats like Twitter and Facebook are designed to be conversational; they reflect a fairly flat model of authority in which voice is given to many people rather than to a few officials or experts. These new formats make it easy to build networks within which new interpretations appear and are tested. In contrast, hierarchical institutions, religious and otherwise, want to build web-sites that function like print or television. They imagine that information only flows one way.

At the end of the twentieth century the World Wide Web was still primarily a location for passive data. Its significance was that it made more information available to more people in searchable formats. The turn of the century marked the rise of what came to be called "Web 2.0." Websites became interactive spaces where the users could do more than consume content; they were able to comment on it, edit it, and add to it. One piece of evidence that individuals and institutions are adapting to the emerging media culture with its flattening of authority is their willingness, perhaps even clamor, for their websites to be venues of conversation and debate rather than mere purveyors of information.

The website of Focus on the Family, a large socially and theologically conservative media ministry that teaches hierarchical family values, is one example of this desire to use new media like old media. The site is visually attractive and filled with images, question-and-answer forums, and data. It is full of top-down advice and information in columns and videos. If you have a concern you can click on "Frequently Asked Questions" and select the question most like your own to get the site writers' counsel. What you cannot do is post your own opinion, disagree with their answers, or for that matter even frame your own questions. Only recently, as their president has begun to blog, has there been any space to respond.

It is not surprising that conservative religious communities who assume that they possess clearly fixed religious truths use new media in ways that privilege the voices of key leaders. However, visits to the websites of established liberal communities and traditions reveal that liberals seem equally slow to embrace the implications of Web 2.0. Emerging religious communities and younger practitioners have been more likely to accept the more conversational implications and possibilities of Web 2.0.

The struggle over how to use new media is also found in the websites maintained by Muslim student groups in the United States. Many are primarily outlets for some authoritative tradition or teacher, usually from abroad. But others are created locally and give voice to young Muslims themselves as they examine what it means for them to be modern, Muslim, and American. These websites are works in progress, spaces in which young Muslims explore their identities, take stands, and respond to each other, in effect using the Web as a place where they can perform their bifurcated identities as Muslim Americans.

Together the authoritative sites, in which foreign imams give direction about proper Muslim life, and the performative sites, where young Muslims, often students, work out their own identities, reflect religion's struggle with the constructive and conversational forms of identity typical of digital culture. The student-run sites adopt the conversational style of digital culture through which individuals network and construct individual religious identities, while the often Saudi-funded sites resist that style in order to maintain an authoritative structure tied to earlier models of communication. Whether this networked and constructed form of religious identity is resisted or embraced, it is a part of the digital culture in which we live as well as a part of contemporary religious life. Such changes point to the question of what organized Islam will look like in the West. Will the mosque, led by a foreign-born and trained cleric, be the dominant expression of organized Muslim life, or are alternative expressions of modernist Islam establishing their own sites and institutions?

Identity construction in and around organized religion

Religion tends to make an absolute claim on identity. To embrace a particular tradition by declaring oneself a Hindu, a Reformed Jew, or a Seventh-day Adventist is to say "this is a central fact of my identity." There is a tension between this absolute identification and the way identity is worked out in digital culture. It was argued in earlier chapters that the linearity of writing resulted in a particular kind of thinking rooted in logical progression. Digitized information seems to function differently. It is subject to easy manipulation and less linear combinations. Sampling, the act of taking bits and pieces of someone else's artistic work, is a central component of creation in the digital world. Originality is not only found in doing something entirely new or in following a single strand to its logical conclusion, but also in putting found and inherited elements together in new ways. How will organized religious communities, ideas, and institutions change if, rather than being central facts of identity, they become elements in the constructed religious identities of individuals?

Hip hop provides an illustration of how identity is constructed in digital culture. Performers play with the elements of what went before, scratching, sampling, and combining to find new resonances and patterns. Hollywood films with titles like 2011's *Cowboys and Aliens* share this approach. They create narrative out of the surprise of combining two familiar but distinct genres. Scholars function in a similar way, finding new knowledge at the intersections of traditionally distinct fields. Many people create religious identity in this way as well. Protestants "sample" forms of Catholic spirituality; Jew-Bus understand themselves to be simultaneously Jewish and Buddhist. Lynn Schofield Clark (2005) demonstrates that many American teens inhabit a complex moral universe that combines Christian symbols with images from the occult and the paranormal.

It can be a challenge for practitioners of organized religions to see their traditions used in this constructive way. They see elements of their traditions sampled by people who make these pieces a part of their individual religious identity in ways that separate the image, practice, or concept from the internal logic and disciplines of the tradition. Yet some established religious communities are moving into this boundary space, attempting to connect with those who draw on the traditions in their constructions of religious lives.

For example, in Denver, Colorado, the historically separatist Mennonite church has assigned pastor Dayvid Graybill to work with a group of urban artists, the majority of whom might be described as "former Mennonites" in that they have given up consistent worship, but continue to be shaped by the tradition in which they grew up. The artists, who have otherwise largely abandoned traditional religious practice while still being shaped by their Mennonite past, call their community Another Way. They gather to eat, drink, share their art and stories, and ponder questions about what sustains ethical and spiritual life. Here a representative of a tradition follows individuals out of the established church, maintaining a connection and creating a ritual space that helps to produce or reinforce individual identity and community around an artistic practice that carries some spiritual valence. However, it's not easy to know how the participants or the denomination understand their connection to Mennonite Christianity.

Rethinking what a "new church start" might look like, United Methodist pastor Jerry Herships established After Hours, Denver. In this "theology pub" a constantly evolving community meets in a bar for theological conversation and networks with more established churches to celebrate communion and provide meals to the homeless in a city park. A wider network follows the organization through social media, responding to invitations to offer prayers and material support to those in need. Both in the bar and in the park, these Methodists stretch what it means to be a congregation.

Nadia Bolz Weber, a Lutheran pastor with a widely read blog and hundreds of Facebook followers, is the designated pastor of Denver's House of All Sinners and Saints. The church is affiliated with the Evangelical Lutheran Church in America (ELCA) and also with the informal "emergent church movement" that deliberately experiments with new models of "church." The boundaries of her congregation are difficult to define. They meet in a borrowed sanctuary. People who have never attended are digitally linked to the congregation and regard it, in some way, as a part of their religious identity. Invited by tweets and Facebook posts to pray for one another, they respond, digitally, that they are doing so.

At the same time, some new religions seek to become more like established religions. The practitioners of Neopaganism often describe themselves as reconnecting with an ancient tradition. Outsiders have questioned the continuity of this practice and, observing their loose organization and marginalized status, often describe Neopaganism as an example of the emergence of a "new" religion. One Neopagan group samples the familiar language of organized religions in their search for legitimacy. Striving to be more organized and established, members of the Living Earth Church sample the language of the still dominant religious tradition in the region, and call themselves a "church," and the leader of their Wiccan practice, Joy Burton, "pastor." Their construction of religious identity points to how they are similar to and different from their Christian neighbors.

The examples above provide on-the-ground illustrations from one city of how established forms of religion can adapt to new ways of being religious and to the way the elements of established religion are sampled by people creating new locations for belief and practice. In some of these examples we see institutional religions adopting new forms and settings for religious practice in order to attract outsiders. In others, the practices or structures of "church" are something that new communities draw on without making the institutional church a part of their conscious practice. In still others, both seem to be going on at once.

Branding as identity construction in religion

In a digital culture, where individual religious consumers are exposed to innumerable religious possibilities, institutional religions have begun to learn the lessons of branding from the world of commercial advertising. The religions see that they need to create clear and inviting images that create a sense of identity. In doing so the institution itself uses media technologies and spaces in a process of identity construction.

In 2011 the Church of Jesus Christ of Latter-day Saints ran a media campaign in the United States. In TV spots and on billboards individuals of diverse ethnicities and social classes engaged in a variety of activities such as working as an artist, riding a motorcycle, or feeding the homeless. Each person proclaimed at the end, "I'm a Mormon," or had this phrase printed below his or her photo (Figure 6.2). The campaign cleverly addressed two slightly conflicting stereotypes about Mormons. It took a religion that has been seen as marginal and exotic, one that is described by some critics as a cult, and presented it as made up of everyday, interesting people. Mormons are also by reputation conservative, a homogeneous community of predominantly white, Republican nuclear families. The "I'm a Mormon" Mormons were, by contrast, much more diverse than the stereotype; they were presented as unique individuals, some of them fairly unconventional. On the ongoing "I'm a Mormon" website you can enter your own gender, age, and ethnicity to discover Mormons in your own demographic. The result is a picture of the Church of Jesus Christ of Latter-day Saints that suggests that, as with the religious practices of other communities, Mormon religious life can be sampled and combined into the diversity of American life.

It is impossible to say what the still inchoate digital culture will mean for organized religion in the long run. We do not know which new practices and institutions will succeed, or which established traditions will struggle and shrink. There will likely continue to be space for religious communities who resist the implications of digital culture, defining themselves in opposition to these changes, though they will likely seem increasingly separatist or counter-cultural. Other

Figure 6.2 Mormon.org billboard

religious communities will experiment with varying degrees of comfort with the new forms of communication and community. Some will see their established communities shrink even as spiritual seekers sample their rich beliefs, images, and practices in constructing more customized religious lives outside organized religion. But it seems likely that, however people are constructing themselves, whatever new forms of religion are emerging, the symbols and practices connected with church, mosque, temple, or synagogue will be a part of the rich stuff that people sample as they formulate their religious identity in the digital age.

Discussion questions

1 What is it about emerging forms of media that makes the mutual relationship between religion and media more obvious?
2 Where do you see established religious communities adapting to new media today? Where do you see them doing this well? What are some of the consequences of religious communities adopting new forms of media without reflecting on how they may be changed by these new media practices?
3 What do we learn about media and religion more generally from reflecting on the way different groups of American Christians have made use of television? How were Evangelicals changed by the development of televangelism? Why were mainline Christians slower to invest in television ministries?
4 What is Web 2.0 and what are its implications for the presence of organized religion on the Web?
5 The chapter suggests that even those who participate in established forms of religion often use it in projects of religious identity construction. Discuss how established religion is sampled, and implications of this practice for the participants and the religious traditions they sample.
6 The reflections that follow look at two religious traditions that are often thought of as new or exotic, and consider how they use media and mediation to be accepted. Thevenin writes about the "I am a Mormon" media campaign, reflecting on how Mormons present themselves. Pike looks at the campaign to have veterans' cemeteries allow the graves of Wiccan soldiers to be marked with the pentacle. What do we learn about religious diversity and inclusion from these examples? What do they teach us about religious identity, and about the performance of that identity in public spaces?

References

Clark, Lynn Schofield (2005) *From Angels to Aliens*, New York: Oxford University Press.
Hoover, Stewart M. (2006) *Religion in the Media Age*, London: Routledge.

Morgan, David (1999) *Protestants and Pictures: Religion, Visual Culture, and the Age of American Mass Production*, New York: Oxford University Press.

Pew Research Center (2011) *Pew Forum on Religion and Public Life*, January 27.

Pike, Sarah (2008) "Religion," in David Morgan, ed. *Key Words in Media, Religion, and Culture*, London: Routledge.

Standage, Tom (2011) "Social Media in the 16th Century: How Luther Went Viral," *The Economist*, Dec 17.

Reflection

Wicca and religious freedom networking in the digital age

Sarah M. Pike

Sgt. Patrick Stewart, a Wiccan, was serving in the US Air Force when the helicopter carrying him was shot down in Afghanistan by Taliban terrorists in 2005. His widow Roberta wanted the US Department of Veterans Affairs (VA) to mark his grave with a pentacle, the Wiccan symbol of a star with five points representing earth, air, water, fire and spirit. The VA had a list of 30 approved religious symbols, but Stewart was told that the pentacle was not one of them and that she would have to go through a long process to get it approved. It turned out that Wiccans had petitioned for the same right years earlier. Their applications had been continually delayed, while other religious groups' symbols were approved more quickly. Stewart contacted Circle Sanctuary, a Wiccan church known for religious freedom advocacy on behalf of Wiccans and other Neopagans. Circle spread the word over its many media and Internet contacts that Wiccan veterans were being unequally treated by the VA.

Circle Sanctuary's "Lady Liberty League," which was founded in the 1980s to promote religious freedom, is highlighted on Circle's website and features a detailed account of what came to be known as the "Veteran Pentacle Quest" (www.circlesanctuary.org/index.php/lady-liberty-league/the-story-of-the-veteran-pentacle-quest.html). Reverend Selena Fox of Circle published several stories on the website from 2005 on, which were picked up by Neopagan blogs like "The Wild Hunt" (http://wildhunt.org) and online news sites like Witchvox.com. Wiccans and other Neopagans were among the first religions to begin networking over the Internet, which offered anonymity as well as a supportive community for those who were afraid of being persecuted for their beliefs. Since the 1990s, Wiccans have used the Internet and other forms of media to promote accurate information about their religion and to counter misrepresentations. The Veteran Pentacle Quest was successful in part because of the widespread appearance of stories on the Internet, which were also picked up by news outlets across the country as varied as *Christianity Today* and the *New York Times*.

Eventually, an organization called Americans United for Separation of Church and State sued the VA on behalf of Circle, alleging religious bias, and settled in US District Court in 2007. The VA approved the pentacle as an official emblem in 2007. Soon afterwards, Roberta Stewart appeared in news stories beside her husband's memorial plaque with its pentacle (http://stewartmemorial.tripod.com/pentaclequest.htm). A full account of the Veteran Pentacle Quest is online at www.circlesanctuary. org, as are photos of veterans' graves marked with pentacles. As one veteran's wife told Fox News, "I like to see our success literally etched in stone, because it will be" (Figure 6.3).

A lively online presence, widespread media coverage, and the eventual victory of the Veteran Pentacle Quest have resulted in greater understanding of Wicca among reporters and the general public, as well as increased openness among Wiccans and other Neopagans about their religious identities. In this and other cases, Wiccans used online networking as well as more traditional media channels to rally support and celebrate their victory.

Figure 6.3 Grave with Wiccan pentacle

Reflection
Advertising that "I'm a Mormon"

Benjamin Thevenin

You might call 2011 the "Mormon Moment," when The Church of Jesus Christ of Latter-day Saints (LDS) was the subject of much public attention. *The Book of Mormon* musical was killing on Broadway and Mitt Romney would soon be the Republican Party's nominee for the presidency. The LDS Church itself entered the conversation about the public perception of Mormons with the "I'm a Mormon" campaign, in which billboards, TV spots, online ads, and a new website mormon.org featured a diverse array of church members, sharing both their unique identities and their shared faith as Mormons.

The ads were ubiquitous on television for months; readers might have caught a few. Each spot would introduce an individual, feature them discussing their careers, families, and passions, and end with them identifying themselves as Mormon. This final declaration was structured to come as a surprise and was a uniting element to a series of ads which featured a pretty eclectic mix of personalities including a physics professor from Vanderbilt University, a professional surfer from Hawaii, and a beekeeper from Italy. This variety presented the LDS people as a diverse group of interesting individuals, people you might already know and like, who happen to be members of the Mormon faith.

One notable example is the TV spot featuring Cassandra Barney, a Utah-based painter and mother. Cassandra's profile is significant because, like many of the ads, it implicitly challenges stereotypical perceptions of Mormons. Cassandra is a spunky artist who paints female matadors "ready to take on whatever comes their way, and do it beautifully." She's also a committed mother of three girls and makes a particular effort to acknowledge her husband's role in her career as an artist: "He … wanted me to pursue this, was really good at picking up the slack, and never said 'Get in there and clean that house!'" Cassandra pushes the boundaries of common representations of LDS women as polygamous wives and bonnet-wearing pioneers. Yet her identity is still recognizably Mormon, anchored in faith and family.

For decades, the LDS Church has used media to answer Jesus' call to "Go ye unto all the world, and preach my gospel to every creature." But something that distinguishes the "I'm a Mormon" campaign from previous public relations efforts is its emphasis on individuals rather than on teachings. While the ads and billboards potentially fulfill an evangelical function, their primary focus is to help the public first get to know and relate to Mormons as people (and often cool ones, at that). Also significant is that these Latter-day Saints are not just the subject of the campaign, but also active participants in its considerable social media presence. All Mormons, together with Cassandra, are invited to use Mormon.org, blogs, YouTube, and Facebook to share their stories and engage in conversations as means of encouraging a greater public understanding of their people, practices, and perspectives. Not only does this mark the LDS Church's venture into the age of crowd-sourced, digital media marketing, but it also puts its faithful at the forefront, a people on a mission to use media to clarify misconceptions, share their own stories, and spread their beliefs.

Part 3

Ethics and esthetics

This closing section of *Media, Religion and Culture: An Introduction* considers how ethical concerns shape the strategies through which religious communities engage news and entertainment media, argues that more attention to how media evoke esthetic responses would deepen our understanding of religion and media, and concludes with three case studies.

Chapter 7: To censor, shape, or engage with media and the arts? examines the ethical concern about media and media content raised from religious perspectives and explores what they suggest about religion and its relationship to the societies in which it is embedded. Using an analysis of American Christianity's varied responses to the movies as a central example, the chapter reviews a variety of strategies which leaders and denominations have adopted including avoidance, censorship, critique and embrace of media. Attention to this variety enriches our understanding of religion's complex relationship to the media worlds in which it is embedded.

Chapter 8: Reading, listening, watching considers how the tools of esthetic analysis, particularly those used in studying literature, music, and film can be applied to the study of religions and their mediations. The approach encourages attention to the material of religion, and to religious practices, giving attention to how they evoke sensual responses.

Chapter 9: Case studies provides three case studies and discussion questions for individual or classroom reflection. They include: the 2005 publication by the Danish newspaper *Jyllands-Posten* of the cartoons depicting the Prophet Muhammad and the ensuing controversy; the development of a Pentecostal film industry in Ghana and Nigeria; and PostSecret, an online site that publishes confessional postcards submitted anonymously. The cases provide an opportunity for readers to apply the understandings of media, religion, and culture that they are developing to concrete examples.

7 To censor, shape, or engage with media and the arts?

Key ideas

- The complex ways that religious leaders and institutions respond to the media worlds they inhabit reflect, in part, their understanding of the moral good and role of religion in society.
- Some religious leaders and institutions welcome new forms of media as an opportunity to better serve their own religious goals or as a potential location for ethical dialog and/or for reflection on the human condition.
- For others, resistance to new forms of media is rooted in a religious resistance to image itself, or in broader moral and ethical concerns about media content and its assumed effects.

Religions have had a mixed relationship with art and media. As argued throughout this book, it is impossible to separate religion from its mediations, which include the expression of religion in art, music, literature, and film. Yet, religions have often been concerned that, while image can lead people toward the sacred, it can also lead them away. After briefly describing this ambivalent relationship between religion and art this chapter looks at the presence of religion as a subject in the movies before turning to consider Christian responses to the cinema, particularly in the United States, as one example of the range of ways in which religious communities have responded to media.

Some of the earliest extant human art that we know of, Paleolithic cave paintings located in France, are religious or spiritual in nature. According to one scholar, "These grottos were probably the first temples and cathedrals. ... Certainly they set the scene for a profound meeting between men and the god-like, archetypal animals that adorn the cavern walls and ceilings" (Armstrong 2005: 32–33). Other powerful esthetic mediations of religion are easy to find. Seek out the great Buddha statue in Bodh Gaya, India, or any of the countless images of the Hindu god Ganesh with his elephant head. Consider the icons of their saints treasured by Greek and Russian Orthodox Christians, or visit the Torah-themed Marc Chagall stained glass windows at Hadassah Medical Center in Jerusalem. Ponder the spare beauty of a New England Quaker meeting house or Istanbul's soaring and ornate Blue Mosque. Art and architecture are primary mediators of religion.

Understanding how the sacred finds expression through art and architecture, through image, sound, and movement expands the description of religion. Yet, for all the evidence that religion is embedded in image, art, and architecture, art evokes a twofold religious anxiety. First, people in some traditions are concerned that the esthetic effort to express those sacred realities within the physical realm will become a substitute for the sacred they are intended to represent. Second, at some level art is a competing space of ritual and life-shaping narratives that like religion may call forth reverie, reflection, and emulation. Religion's complicated relationship with the cinema provides one illustration of the range of ways that religion relates to art and media more broadly.

Religious images have such power that religious conflict is often expressed through attacks by one religious group on the images and objects that mediate other religions. Indeed, the word *iconoclast* is rooted in the destruction of religious images. Near the Roman Forum you can visit a Christian church built triumphantly within the columns of a collapsed Roman temple. When fourteenth-century Ottoman Turks captured the region of Cappadocia in present-day Turkey, they scratched out the eyes on the paintings of Christian saints in order to counteract the power of these images (Figure 7.1). During the sixteenth century, Christian followers of the Radical Reformation destroyed stained glass windows and art that they regarded as blasphemous.

The theological, political, and esthetic conflicts that led to the destruction of religious art and architecture continue in more recent times. Seeing some forms of popular culture as a competing source of ritual and meaning, religious leaders sometimes seek to control or destroy them. In areas of Afghanistan controlled by the Taliban, music and movies are banned, in part for their capacity to carry with them Western values. When rock and roll emerged in the United States,

Figure 7.1 Frescoes, Turkey

clergy preached against it as "the devil's music" or, noting its rooting in African American musical forms, used the racist term "jungle music" to describe it. To this day conservative Christian congregations sometimes destroy CDs and DVDs they find immoral or blasphemous. The publication of cartoons of the Prophet Muhammad in the Danish newspaper *Jyllands-Posten* in 2005, and subsequently elsewhere in Europe and the United States, can be seen as a reversal of this pattern. The secular society asserts its moral power over religion, not by destroying religious art, but by publishing images that some Muslims regard as blasphemous.

The development of the movies, both as a technology and as a set of narrative and visual genres, happened fairly quickly, moving from quirky innovation to popular entertainment over a period of just 25 to 30 years. Considering how religious communities expressed their attitudes, and sometimes anxieties, about the new medium helps to illustrate the range of ways that religious communities reflect on mediation more generally.

Religion in the movies

The movie camera was developed simultaneously by the Lumière brothers in France and Thomas Edison in the United States in the late 1880s. By the turn of the twentieth century the cinema was becoming a common public entertainment. Between 1913 and 1916, 21,000 movie theaters opened in the United States (Johnston 2000: 20). While the earliest viewers were fascinated by simply watching movement on film, film-makers quickly seized on the new medium as a way to tell stories and began to adapt the popular literary genres for subject matter, and the early public screenings included westerns, romances and biblical tales.

Motion pictures continued to be a location for religion. It is reported that films about the life of Jesus were among the first films shown in the United States (Mahan) and religion continued to be a subject in Hollywood. Although much of that work has been lost, some silent-era religious films, like Cecil B. DeMille's (1923) *Ten Commandments*, are still available. Later Technicolor and big budgets enabled Hollywood "Biblical spectaculars" like *The Robe* (1953) and DeMille's return to the Decalogue with his 1956 *The Ten Commandments*.

Americans are not the only ones to make the cinema a location of religion. Europeans and Africans also turn to Christian subject matters in films such as Danish director Carl Theodor Dreyer's *The Passion of Joan of Arc* (1928) and Cheick Sissoko of Mali's *La Genese* (1999). Buddhist content and sensibility are evident in films from a number of countries, with Korean director Bae Yong-Kyun's *Why has Bodhi-Dharma Left for the East?* (1989) a notable example. While Muslims object to the portrayal of Muhammad, the Islamic faith and worldview are evident in films, perhaps most notably those from Iran such as Majid Majid's *Children of Heaven* (1997) and Abbas Kiarostami's *Taste of Cherry*, which won the *Palme d'Or* at Cannes the same year.

In the first decade of the twentieth century Dadasaheb Phalke wrote about his experience in a Bombay theater watching a film called *The Life of Christ*.

While the life of Christ was rolling fast before my physical eyes I was mentally visualizing the Gods, Shri Krishna, Shri Ramchandra, then Gokul and Ayodhya. I was gripped by a strange spell. … Could we the sons of India, ever be able to see the Indian images on the screen?

(Phalke in Mitchell and Plate 2007: 25)

Phalke would make the first feature-length motion picture produced in India, *Raja Harishchandra* (1913), drawing its narrative from the Sanskrit epic the *Ramayana*. He went on to establish the Indian film industry that has become known as "Bollywood," a vast industry informed by Hindu esthetics and worldview and often explicitly populated by the Hindu gods (Figure 7.2).

People working within the film industry, with varying degrees of religious sensibility, create theatrical movies about religious subjects. Examples include films like Martin Scorsese's *Kundun* (1997), which sought to express a Buddhist sensibility in telling the story of the Dalai Lama. The presence of religion in film is of course not limited to movies with obvious religious subjects or those made with pious intent. Religious images and figures appear in films for a number of reasons, including the criticism of religion or the provision of a visual language to evoke particular emotions or discuss particular concerns. They include exploitation films like Joseph Guzman's *Nude Nuns with Big Guns* (2010) in which corrupt, drug-dealing priests provide the backdrop for an action adventure comedy, and films that draw on implicit or overt religious themes and images

Figure 7.2 Shree Ganesh movie poster

in more complicated ways to explore moral questions. This is often seen in horror films like *Rosemary's Baby* (1968) that use religious images, characters, or language to explore the question of evil.

Religious responses to the movies

Though religion has been a consistent subject of the movies, religious communities were both intrigued and apprehensive about the new medium and its content. The range of their early responses provides a clue as to the complexities of the relationship between religion and media.

For some, the movies were a godsend. In 1910 the Rev. Herbert Jump wrote a pamphlet titled *The Religious Possibilities of the Motion Picture*. While acknowledging a widespread religious "prejudice against motion pictures," Jump argued that this relatively new medium might serve religion in a beneficial way. He described how a few churches were beginning to provide screenings of films as a form of wholesome entertainment and how images of the "holy land" were being used in religious education. He imagined that filmed presentations of stories from the Bible or church history might be used in religious education and concluded that

> the crowning possibility of the motion picture, though, is its usefulness to the preacher as he proclaims moral truth. It will provide the element of illustration for his discourse far better than it can be provided by the spoken word. It will make his gospel vivid, pictorial, dramatic, and above all, interesting. The motion picture preacher will have crowded congregations, not because he is sensational but because he is appealing to human nature.
>
> (Jump in Mitchell and Plate 2007: 23)

While religious leaders like Jump embraced the possibilities of the movies, others expressed moral qualms about the content of the movies. Concerned about film's capacity to illustrate and encourage immoral behavior, religious critics raised alarm about the growth of the cinema. As "talkies" emerged, R.G. Burnett and E.D. Martell wrote *The Devil's Camera*, a sensationalist religious warning about the social dangers of the movies. They offered an account of "a school boy and a school girl [who are] ... 'film fans,' steeped in the artificial sentimentality of the modern screen, familiar with the whole sordid concoction of adultery, deception and murder." After the boy and girl leave a London theater, the boy stabs and murders the girl.

> The lad was put on trial for his life; but he ought not to have stood alone in the dock. What of those who, for the lowest of all human ends, had exploited his immature imagination with their screen crimes? ... Nothing is sacred. ... Our very civilization is at stake. The cinema, as at present debased, is the Hun of the modern world.
>
> (Burnett and Martell in Mitchell and Plate 2007: 33, 34)

In 1936, while acknowledging that "good motion pictures are capable of exercising a profoundly moral influence," Pope Pius XI expressed similar though less sensationalist reservations about film's potential to affect people's moral sensibilities. In an encyclical letter supporting the American Bishops' establishment of the Legion of Decency and its role in establishing the Hollywood Production Code, the pope wrote:

> The power of the motion picture consists in this: that it speaks by means of vivid and concrete imagery, which the mind takes in with enjoyment and without fatigue. … Everyone knows what damage is done to the soul by bad motion pictures. They are occasions of sin; they seduce young people along the way of evil by glorifying the passions; they show life under a false light; they cloud ideals; … They are capable also of creating prejudices among individuals, misunderstandings among nations, among social classes, and among entire races.
>
> (*Vigilanti Cura*, in Mitchell and Plate 2007: 39)

A range of religious strategies

It is possible to think of the movies themselves as a form of religion. Some see the experience of going to the movie theater, sitting in the dark, and being engaged by mythic stories as itself a form of religious ritual (Lyden 2003). Certainly the responses of some religious groups and leaders to the movies suggest that they understand them to be a competing source of powerful and compelling stories.

By no means do these anxieties tell the entire story of how religious people have thought about the movie industry. Those who are largely at peace with the wider culture see at least most movies as relatively innocuous expressions of popular culture. Some religious voices recognized that movies can provide reflections on significant social concerns even when they do not overtly address religious topics. Esthetically inclined religious critics see that film can have the power to give expression to the human condition in ways that can instruct the religious viewer. Where this is so, conversation about film provides an opportunity for dialog with wider cultural issues and ideas.

Vibrant examples of these various strategies can be seen in the response of American religious communities to the movies. Some religious communities *avoided* contact with movies and other forms of popular culture as part of a wider strategy of separatist religious identity, others were quick to *adopt* the new medium, some attempted to *control* or shape their content, and still others entered into *reflection on* or *dialog with* the world of film. These strategies are not mutually exclusive; individuals and groups move among them and may practice them simultaneously.

Avoidance

For those who share Burnett and Martell's sense that the movie camera is the tool of the devil, the possibility that film's power over the imagination can be harnessed to tell religious stories is overshadowed by anxiety about the potentially negative influence of movies and the industry that produces them. Those in this tradition often follow a strategy of avoidance. For American Protestants in the holiness traditions that developed prior to the American Civil War, personal morality and the avoidance of worldly distractions are an important expression of the search for religious perfection. Their religious identity is expressed as much in the Christian witness of things they do *not* do as in their acts of piety, charity, and service; thus, as with strictures against dancing or the use of alcohol, avoidance of the movies is regarded as an expression of their Christian faith. From such a perspective, it is not simply that particular movies have bad content. For these religious practitioners going to the movies means participating in a culture that is indolent, choosing a cultural narrative over a religious narrative, and exalting a shallow celebrity culture.

The National Legion of Decency, formed in the 1930s by Roman Catholic bishops, combined a strategy of censorship for the protection of the community with one of avoidance as a primary expression of religious identity. The Legion was involved in developing the Production Code described below that sought to control the content of films. At the same time their original membership pledge read:

> I condemn all indecent and immoral motion pictures, and those which glorify crime or criminals. I promise to do all that I can to strengthen public opinion against the production of indecent and immoral films, and to unite with all who protest against them. I acknowledge my obligation to form a right conscience about pictures that are dangerous to my moral life. I pledge myself to remain away from them. I promise, further, to stay away altogether from places of amusement which show them as a matter of policy.

Pietistic practices such as these have become far less common among contemporary American Christians, though they continue among some groups. As the holiness traditions adapted to the surrounding culture they have become more open to previously banned activities, often moving from total avoidance to standards of moderation. This move toward a greater participation in the wider society led to a gradual softening of the stricture against attending the movies.

Adoption

A contrasting response to that of the avoiders can be seen in that of the adopters who embraced the new medium as a form through which religion could be expressed. Some, like Jump and Phalke, were quick to see that the gods, their saints and followers might appear in visual form on the movie screen. Further, religiously oriented film-makers could use the medium to tell contemporary tales aligned with religious values and worldview.

There are a variety of contemporary expressions of the effort to adopt film to tell religious stories. As Jump hoped in 1910, some pastors and religious educators incorporate film into the worship and educational life of congregations using secular movies to illustrate religious claims. The previous chapter looked at the development of religious television, which brought worship and religious conversation into people's homes. There is a ready market in churches and synagogues for short films with religious themes.

For some film-makers, who may or may not identify with particular religious communities, movies can be a location to explore religious and theological questions. Ingmar Bergman, the questioning son of a stern Swedish pastor, often made films that ponder a dark Christian theological world, as in *The Seventh Seal* (1957), with its emblematic image of death playing chess with the protagonist. More recently, Terrence Malick's *The Tree of Life* (2011) uses film to visualize a world infused with religious meaning and picture the inhabitants who strive, or do not strive, to experience the sacredness of creation.

Mel Gibson famously brought his own pre-Vatican II traditionalist Catholicism to the screen in *The Passion of the Christ* (2004). The violence and radical atonement theology of the film were debated vigorously by both supporters and opponents. Less financially and critically successful was celebrity Scientologist John Travolta's effort to bring Scientology founder L. Ron Hubbard's novel *Battlefield Earth* (2000) to the screen.

While the celebrity of film-makers like Travolta and Gibson allowed them to occasionally produce movies that reflect their religious worldview within the Hollywood system, others with less clout who wanted to work more consistently in a religious mode have moved away from the predominantly secular movie-making industry to create separate production companies and distribution systems within which they could make religiously motivated movies. One such company is Affirm Films, a wing of Sony Pictures, that most famously released Sean McNamara's successful *Soul Surfer* (2011), the story of a young surfer whose Christian faith helps her recover from a shark attack and return to surfing. Others with an apocalyptic theology came together to produce *Left Behind* (2001) and its sequels, all starring former child star Kirk Cameron. The films explore the idea of a "rapture" in which believers are taken to heaven and non-believers left behind to face a "tribulation," and were widely promoted within the Evangelical community. There have been many such low-budget efforts by people of a variety of faiths. Qasim Basir's *Mooz-Lum* (2011) uses a melodramatic form to tell the story of Muslim life in America. First promoted through social media, the film saw a brief theatrical release. These films often depend on such alternative distribution strategies and are promoted within particular religious communities.

For the religiously inspired Hollywood film-makers described above, and others like them, movies are an outlet for the religious imagination. These film-makers, however, have generally used their celebrity to make room for religious projects in a largely secular industry, or created alternative structures of production and distribution at the edges of the industry. In Nigeria and Ghana an independent industry has developed that produces movies in inexpensive video formats that reflect the Pentecostal worldview of the region. Films like Kenneth Nnebue's

Living in Bondage (1992) established a tradition of cinematic storylines in which Pentecostal Christians are victorious over those who maintain traditional African religious practices.

Controlling the movies: censorship and the Production Code

By the early twentieth century, evangelical Protestants and Roman Catholics began to participate more fully in the wider society in the United States. For many, the separatist religious strictures urging people to entirely avoid the movies eased and began to be replaced by other strategies. They came to see the cinema as a potentially acceptable place of wholesome entertainment or reflection on society and the human condition. Nonetheless, religious leaders and institutions continued to have reservations about the power of the movies to shape personal and public morality. These reservations led them to strategies that attempted to influence or control the content of the movies. This theoretical acceptance of the movies was constrained by concerns about content, which has been the dominant religious response to the movies in the United States.

Though the religious sensibility that suggested that the movies were to be avoided has become, for most American Christians, a distant memory, religious institutions or individuals often seek to use their own moral and political influence to affect or control the content of the movies. A concern for what Pope Pius called "the passions" often leads to religiously based criticism of the movies focused on concerns around individual morality, particularly in terms of sex, violence, and crime. A wider social critique is expressed by Christians who share Pius's concern that the movies "are capable also of creating prejudices among individuals, misunderstandings among nations, among social classes, and among entire races" (Mitchell and Plate 2007: 38). Religious critique of the movies also includes misgivings about the way that popular entertainment sometimes draws on common prejudices, devalues women, marginalizes already oppressed minorities, and celebrates a life of consumption that rests on inequality and exploitation. Certainly many of these concerns are shared by other social critics.

While some religious communities were beginning to regard moviegoing as a potentially acceptable activity in the teens and early 1920s, the religious shared with many others a sense of alarm about the licentiousness of some films. Legislators across the United States were debating movie censorship. While it was not only religious people and institutions raising concerns about movie content, much of the concern was framed in religious language. Because the US Supreme Court had earlier ruled that movies were not constitutionally protected free speech, there was a real possibility that each community might set its own standards, each title might have to be submitted to multiple boards of review, each of which might ask for revisions, and that theater owners and movie producers might face prosecution in more than one jurisdiction. This was a daunting situation for the film industry.

In 1922 the Hollywood studios turned to former head of the Republican Party and Presbyterian layperson Will H. Hays to advise them and clean up the film industry's public image. By 1930 Roman Catholic leaders proposed a binding code and in 1934, fearing government censorship, the studios adopted this proposal for self-censorship and the "Hays Code" set limits on film content until 1968.

The Code set out three "Guiding Principles:"

1   No picture shall be produced that will lower the moral standards of those who see it. Hence the sympathy of the audience should never be thrown to the side of crime, wrongdoing, evil, or sin.
2   Correct standards of life, subject only to the requirements of drama and entertainment, shall be presented.
3   Law, natural or human, shall not be ridiculed, nor shall sympathy be created for its violation.

The role of religion in shaping the Code can be seen in its incorporation of the doctrines of sin and natural law. The Principles were followed by a discussion of "Particular Applications." Among the many Particular Applications were limits on how sexual attraction could be portrayed, emphasizing support for the institution of heterosexual marriage, as well as limits on nudity, costuming, and the presentation of the body. There were also limits on the depiction of crime and criminals, requiring that crime always be punished. Religion was protected with restrictions against the ridicule of religion and the portrayal of religious leaders as villains or comic figures; moreover, religious services should be "carefully and respectfully handled."

The 1950s and '60s were a period of considerable social change in the United States. Normative values about sex, race, and religion were liberalizing and film-makers would increasingly challenge Hays-office rulings on movies that reflected the changing culture. Struggles over film censorship came to a head in 1952, when the distributors of the 1948 Roberto Rossellini film *L'amore* (*The Miracle*) defended the film in the US Supreme Court, establishing the principle that films were a form of constitutionally protected speech. With this decision, the argument that the Hays Code defended Hollywood against government censorship was weakened. By the end of the 1960s the combination of new understandings about free speech and changing social values led to the collapse of the regulation of which films could be produced and distributed in the United States. But it did not bring an end to the religious community's wariness of the movies.

Protest

Where efforts to ban particular movies have failed, religious groups have sometimes turned to acts of public protest. There is a long history of picketing theaters to shame patrons and theater managers and sometimes to elicit conversation. For those whose religious identity was constructed in opposition to the wider society, movies and other media are simply the presenting face of a wider culture that they reject. Various conservative Christian groups argued for boycotts of movies ranging from *The Da Vinci Code* (2006) to *The Hobbit* (2012). This sometimes brings them into coalition with other social reformers. The protest of films deemed pornographic, for instance, brought Christian conservatives together with religious and secular feminists.

Other coalitions come together to oppose movies that they regard as blasphemous. One notable example of a movie that drew strong objections was *The Last Temptation of Christ*, the 1988 film by Martin Scorsese that explores what the life of Jesus might have been like had he not been crucified. While Scorsese argued that the film explored the doctrine of the incarnation, Catholics, Orthodox Christians, Evangelicals, and representatives from other denominations protested the film. In Paris the protests included the burning of a theater, a throwback to the desire to obliterate art regarded as blasphemous that emerges in many traditions at various points in their history.

Rating systems

Yet another strategy, also rooted in concern about the movies' content and influence, was the development of ratings systems. Recognizing that the US courts increasingly treated movies as a form of art protected by standards of free speech, the development of motion picture rating systems provided guidance to audiences about a film's content without seeking to ban the particular film. Religious communities were often involved in developing or supporting rating systems. Religiously motivated raters sought to differentiate between films that they considered appropriate and those they deemed disturbing or morally dangerous.

Following the collapse of the Hays Code, the Motion Picture Association of America (MPAA), under the leadership of Jack Valenti, developed a rating system, established in 1968 and modified slightly over the years. Religious leaders from the National Council of Churches and National Catholic Council participated in the development of the standards. The MPAA ratings are not meant to be a judgment of the quality of the movie but of its suitability for particular audiences. There have been some changes over the years, both in the rating categories themselves and in what content would produce a particular rating. Raters look at the amount of profanity, nudity, drug use, sex, violence, and what the MPAA calls "mature" or "adult" themes in a film in considering how to place it in one of five categories. Movies rated "G" are judged to be appropriate for a general audience, and all ages can be admitted into the theater. "PG" indicates that parental guidance is called for, as some of the film's material, according to the raters, may not be appropriate for children. "PG-13" indicates a stronger caution to parents, especially parents with children under the age of 13. "R" indicates that children under 17 cannot be admitted to the theater to see the film unless they are accompanied by an adult, while a rating of "NC-17" means that no children under 17 are to be admitted.

Wanting to give expression to their own worldview and ethical concerns, some religious communities have established their own ratings. Perhaps the best known of these was established by The National Legion of Decency to guide Catholic viewers. The system made distinctions between films which were "A: Morally unobjectionable," "B: Morally objectionable in part," or "C: Condemned by the Legion of Decency." Those rated A were further subdivided between those that were "suitable for all audiences," "suitable for adults and adolescents," "suitable for adults only," or "for adults with reservations." For groups like the Legion of Decency, it was important to have ratings more explicitly rooted in their own religious framework.

Other religious groups also established their own rating systems. Where the avoiders have argued that all movies are implicated in a system of moral illusion, the religious leaders and communities involved in rating films acknowledged that there were movies that do no harm and even some which are morally uplifting or otherwise serve positive ethical and social goals. Overall, the religious groups' strategies of ratings, censorship, and avoidance reflect a suspicion of the Hollywood dream machine as a source of seductive illusions.

Theological reflection on and dialogue with the movies

A shifting of attitudes toward culture, and a readiness to engage with it in new ways, can be seen in the decision of the Catholic bishops in the 1960s to replace the Legion of Decency with the Film and Broadcast Office of the United States Conference of Catholic Bishops. Where the Legion had focused on warning viewers away from things that the raters thought they should not see, the new Film and Broadcast Office was charged with a wider conversation with and about the movies. Though the Office continues a Catholic rating system, ratings are part of a broader strategy of film reviews that model ways of thinking about movies as part of a larger Catholic conversation with culture. In doing so the Film and Broadcast Office moved toward the strategy of esthetic, social, and theological dialog with the movies.

The greater openness to the movies suggests that religious communities have come to understand themselves to be in an esthetic and ethical conversation with culture. Culture is not inherently fallen. Approached in this way, the movies are a location for reflection on the beautiful, the good, and their opposites. While such religious viewers may have concerns about particular films, they see the movies in general as a form of art to be engaged with.

For some religious critics, film primarily provides illustration of theological arguments that they are making. But others go beyond this to tease out the theological implications that are internal to particular films, valuing films and film-makers for their unique worldviews and artistic accomplishments. James M. Wall, for many years the editor and publisher of the progressive Christian journal *The Christian Century*, is one who models a public conversation about religion and film that is thoughtfully about the esthetic nature of film.

Film-makers are often frustrated or perplexed by their religious critics. Faced with religious boycotts, negative ratings, or religiously motivated complaints that they only produce films that celebrate a culture of violence, shallow sexuality and consumption, film-makers often respond that religious leaders fail to understand the economic and esthetic complexities within which they work. Further, film-makers suggest, their religious critics fail to turn out to support films whose values they might have celebrated. Attempting to respond to this criticism, some religiously motivated film critics and academic and religious media professionals have tried to create opportunities for more conversation between the church and film-makers. One expression of this has been to establish religious juries at a number of international film festivals. Organized by the World Catholic Association for Communication and the equivalent Protestant body, the International Interchurch Film Organization, these juries review the films in the official competition at international film festivals at Cannes, Berlin, Montreal, and a number of other cities. They give an award to the film that most represents what the jurors understand to be religious and human values and use the award to create conversations with film-makers and other critics about how esthetic and theological interests might come together.

Media education and activism

Another dialogical strategy that religious groups have used in engaging with film and television has been that of media education, with the participants generally recognizing the way in which media, religion, and culture interact and overlay each other. Assuming that media are deeply implicated in social sins such as sexism, racism, consumption, and stereotyping, religious educators have responded by attempting to teach the consumers of mass media, particularly young people, about the content, narrative, and economic structures of mass media. Groups like the World Alliance of Christian Communication also work with reporters and editors in developing countries to encourage alternative voices.

The media education approach shares the sense of some of the groups described above that film and other forms of media are powerful shapers of the imagination. However, the media educators differ from other religious critics of media in two ways. Their ethical concern is focused less on individual piety and more on social issues. Further, the avoiders and raters described above function as though people, particularly young people, are passive viewers who absorb the values, assumptions, and prejudices of whatever they watch, and who therefore need to be protected from negative media. In contrast, the media education movement teaches "active viewing" that encourages viewers to identify the assumed values of media entertainments, ask who benefits from those narrative assumptions, and bring those values into dialog with their own. These religiously motivated efforts to understand and critique the values embedded in popular narratives and advertising have been paralleled by more secular efforts within the public schools. Particularly in Canada, a strong media education movement has developed among public educators. A long-standing example of media education work in the United States can be seen in that of the Center for Media Literacy, an organization first launched by religious communities that now functions as a non-aligned not-for-profit.

Looking at the range of ways that religious leaders and communities have engaged with the movies, it appears that religion's relationship to the arts reflects both a recognition that religion's work is dependent on art and media and the recognition that art forms also serve other systems of value and community. The varied strategies through which religious communities engage with the movies reflect differing theological assumptions about the role of religion in society and the possibility that the good and the beautiful may be found outside as well as inside religion.

Discussion questions

1 How have art and architecture, and attacks upon them, been used to express religious and power relationships? Identify examples of this from the chapter or your own observation.

2 What concerns have led some religious communities to avoid, or to seek to control, the movies? What values and assumptions are expressed in the Production Code and the current rating system?

3 What strategies have other religious communities developed to adopt the movies as a tool for religious practice or education? Can you think of particular good or bad examples of this?

4 What is theological film criticism, and what are its goals? What is the goal of media education, and why have religious communities been interested in this approach?

5 In the following reflection, "Muslim Monsters," Shafi reflects on the film *300* (2007) and discusses the response of Iranians to the film's portrayal of ancient Persia. What is the effect of repeatedly portraying a particular people as monstrous? Do you think these extreme portrayals contribute to prejudice against Muslims?

6 Campbell's reflection considers the development of a kosher cell phone system to serve ultra-Orthodox Jews. What does this example teach us about the religiously motivated anxieties about media and their content, and about their appeal? What does it suggest about how religion can shape media?

References

Armstrong, Karen (2005) *A Short History of Myth,* New York: Cannongate Books.

Johnston, Robert K. (2000) *Reel Spirituality: Theology and Film in Dialogue,* Grand Rapids: Baker Academic.

Lyden, John C. (2003) *Film as Religion: Myths, Morals and Rituals,* New York: New York University Press.

Mahan, Jeffrey H. (2002) "Celuloid Savior: Jesus in the Movies," *Journal of Religion and Film,* Vol. 1, April.

Mitchell, Jolyon and S. Brent Plate, eds. (2007) *The Religion and Film Reader,* New York: Routledge.

Reflection
Koshering the cell phone

Heidi A. Campbell

In March 2005 MIRS Communication, an Israeli wireless company, announced the launch of a cellular phone designed specifically for the ultra-Orthodox Jewish community. The idea for such a phone began in 2004 when ultra-Orthodox rabbis and community members became concerned that cell phones might be enabling immoral content to infiltrate the community. Key to these concerns was the transformation of the cell phone from a simple communication device to one knitting social networking, communication, and entertainment options. The rise of 3G phones in Israel meant people now had easy access to problematic media like the Internet and mainstream media content.

This raised some concerns that the cell phone might also encourage more privatized communication, that was not as easily monitored by parents or religious leaders. This was highly problematic for a community that tries to keep strict boundaries between the sacred and secular world and avoid any contact with any images or content that could encourage sinful thoughts or behaviors. This led to a lengthy negotiation process between a group of Rabbis, who later became known as the Rabbinical Council for Communication Affairs, and a number of Israeli cell phone providers. Eventually MIRS agreed to produce a "kosher phone," a reconditioned first-generation phone where Internet access, SMS text messaging, and video and voice mail application were stripped or disabled. This was coupled with community-specific calling plans that made it very cheap to call other kosher phones and created penalties for calling outside this community network or using the phone on Shabbat. These phones are visibly marked with a stamp signifying approval by the Rabbinical Committee, similar to the symbol found on kosher food products.

Only these phones were seen as "kosher," meaning approved or acceptable under rabbinical, religious law, for devout religious Jews, and the launch was coupled with a media campaign linking use of the device as symbolic of one's religious devotion and faithfulness to the boundaries of the community (Campbell 2010). As one ultra-Orthodox journalist wrote about this campaign, "*Maran verabonon* (masters and sages) defined the battle for kosher communication as an existential battle, a battle for the soul, and that every effort must be made to insure its success." Several years on, a number of other Israeli phone providers offer their own versions of the kosher phone, sold in shops only in ultra-Orthodox neighborhoods

Figure 7.3 Orthodox Jewish man using cell phone

endorsed by specific rabbis and coming with a special phone prefix so that even one's phone number becomes a marker as to whether or not one honored the Rabbinical edict. The kosher cell phone has become a symbol of ultra-Orthodox values of honoring those in authority and living a lifestyle defined by constraining behaviors that "draw a tight fence around the Torah" so that the individual and the community do not fall into sin. It also highlights how conservative religious communities may be motivated to innovate and cultivate technologies in light of their values, rather than outright rejecting them, if they are seen as valuable resources but potentially problematic in their current form (Figure 7.3).

Reference

Campbell, Heidi A. (2010) *When Religion Meets New Media*, Abingdon: Routledge.

Reflection
Muslim monsters
Sophia Shafi

The visions created about individuals outside one's own social group can be highly instructive, providing insights about both the perceiver and how they construct the bodies of others, whether real or imagined. The representation of Muslims in Hollywood is such a case. As documented in the work of scholars like Jack Shaheen, Ella Shohat, and Robert Stam, Muslim villains are common fixtures in movies. Muslim monsters—characters who exhibit non-human and, at times, terrifying attributes—are part of the history of film as well.

The movie *300* (2007), which grossed over $500 million at the box office, is one of the recent films that includes these monsters. It is based on Frank Miller's popular 1998 graphic novel about an epic battle between the Spartans and the Persians. With a few additions made by the film's director, Zach Snyder, *300* is an almost frame-by-frame movie version of the text. The film fictionalizes a famous battle that took place in 480 BCE between the Persians and an alliance of Greek city-states that included the Spartans. In *300*, this battle is transformed into an argument that the Christian and modern West must subdue and civilize the Islamic and pre-modern East. This conflict between the West and Islam begins with the first scenes, in which Persia is described as a "beast" that will devour the West if it is not stopped. The Persians are a collection of deformed hunchbacks, giants, sexual deviants, and other frights. Although the film is set in ancient times, Persians represent the existential threat of Islam, a danger expressed in imagery including Orientalist costume and references to the barbarian East (Figure 7.4).

The Persians of *300* are monsters suffering from a variety of racial and sexual degeneracies, many of them situated in medieval fantasies about Muslim bodies. Xerxes, the Persian king, towers over the Spartan king Leonidas like the giants of medieval tales who dwarfed Christian knights. Xerxes serves as a tableau of a long list of medieval tropes about Muslims—they are giants; they have black, purple, or brown skin; they are bisexual; they have sex with boys; they are inhuman. Beside Xerxes, Persian monsters in the film include the 10-foot tall giants with lobster claws and filed teeth, giants with missing arms and metal prosthetics, and the disfigured lesbians and other Persians who occupy Xerxes' harem.

Film critics have identified the grossly inaccurate ways in which Persians are represented, including the characterization of Xerxes as a

Figure 7.4 300 movie poster

cross-dressing gay man. As film reviewer Dana Stephens put it, "The Persian commander, the god-king Xerxes [Rodrigo Santoro] is a towering, bald club fag with facial piercings, kohl-rimmed eyes, and a disturbing predilection for making people kneel before him." Other reviewers have noted, for instance, the way the Persians are depicted as an army of freaks and monsters.

Iranians did not appreciate the film's treatment of Xerxes or of Persians in general. A cultural adviser to then President Ahmadinejad characterized *300* as psychological warfare and the government's UNESCO representative filed a complaint with that organization. Iranian expatriates voiced similar objections, criticizing the movie for its mischaracterization of ancient Persia as well as what was viewed as gross racial and cultural stereotyping.

The sequel to *300* is due to be released in the spring of 2014, focusing on Xerxes and his rise to power, the events leading up to and following the Battle of Thermopylae, and the Battle of Artemisium. One can only wonder what horrors will await.

8 Reading, listening, watching

Key ideas

- The esthetic experience of religion is rooted in our bodily responses. In order to interpret religion and media as bodily experience we need to understand the literary, visual, and aural "texts" (including movies, television programs, novels, newspapers, magazines, music, video games, and websites as well as more traditional religious art and architecture) through which religious and secular media evoke human responses.
- Esthetic interpretations deepen our description and understanding of both religious art and religion itself.

Understanding media, religion, and culture requires paying attention to the material "stuff" of religion, to religious texts, physical and digital spaces, and the sounds that give religion a voice, as well as to what people do with this stuff. Without a clear picture of the material, we are unlikely to understand what people are doing with it. Consider, for instance, the elaborate carvings of saints in the *Convento e Igreja de São Francisco* (Convent and Church of Saint Francis) in the city of Salvador, Brazil. Many people describe it as a beautiful example of early eighteenth-century Portuguese-inspired religious architecture and call attention to the exuberant gold leaf that gilds the multitude of carvings and statues of Christian saints and angels. A more careful examination, however, reveals that many of these statues are distorted. Faces appear to be anguished. Female saints appear to be pregnant. Cherubim have enlarged sexual organs. Attention to these surprising details might lead us to ask who carved these statues. This "Portuguese" church was built by African slave labor and the carvings done by enslaved artisans. Tourists who merely tick it off as one more of many churches that they will visit during their trip are likely to miss the slave resistance built into the church. And if they miss that, they are likely to misunderstand the complex relationship of Afro-Brazilians to the religion of their oppressors.

This chapter is designed to encourage readers to read, listen, and watch more carefully as they engage with particular material expressions of religion. Interesting and informative interpretations of religious images or objects, the ways that participants use them, and their contribution to creating religious worlds rest on clear descriptions of the mediations themselves. In this esthetic approach we seek to describe, culturally locate, and reflect on particular religious objects, spaces and actions. What, for example, might an *object* such as a calligraphied Qur'an passed down within a family or a *location* such as the website of a Hindu monastery on the island of Kauai tell us about the religious traditions that produced them and the traditions' interaction with culture and media? What does an *action* such as a Jewish mother's ritual lighting of Shabbat candles or the posting of a confession on the PostSecret website reveal about a religious world? What does a *sound* such as the "keen," or vocal lament, at a pre-Christian Celtic funeral or the music of a Muslim punk band like Britain's Alien Kulture tell us about the religious experience of a people? Esthetic analysis helps us more fully describe and experience these particular expressions and then see how they fit into broader patterns, rhythms, and genres. These approaches are sometimes described as the "close reading" of the mediations of religion.

No single esthetic form or practice fully explains a religion. Religions in which sacred texts are important also have spaces and rituals. So a full picture of a religion requires that we attend to the range of esthetic experiences of the practitioners, that we see its spaces, read its texts, hear its sounds, and smell its smells. No student of religion has the full range of skills to interpret every aspect of the material and practice of religion. Scholars, like practitioners themselves, may have physical or sensual limitations that constrain their experience of the religion; they may find more personal satisfaction in some forms than others, or have the training to see some aspects of a religion and not others. No individual experience or portrait of a religion is in this sense complete. Yet the careful student seeks to develop the critical skills needed to provide as full a picture as possible.

Developing critical skills

The abstract painter Jackson Pollock, who lived in the first half of the twentieth century, was famous for dripping paint onto huge canvases. People who have not honed the critical tools that it takes to understand Pollock's experiments with color and form sometimes dismiss the work with a statement like "My five-year-old could do that." To take another example, when people say about a science fiction film or romantic novel "They are all the same," it is often because they lack the skills or interest to see how particular films or novels create variations within these familiar patterns. Similarly, when someone says that all Muslims are the same, it is likely because that person has not closely observed the varieties of Islamic practice or considered the complex way in which religions participate in the struggles and assumptions of particular cultures and time periods.

The typical readers of this book have probably already taken classes on literature, art, film, or music, where they developed tools of humanistic description and interpretation, and classes on philosophy, rhetoric, or communications designed to sharpen critical thinking. These skills contribute to the "close reading" of the mediations of religion. They allow the observer to describe more clearly the particular mediation of religion, therefore offering a more nuanced interpretation and, in turn, deepening the observer's esthetic experience. Bringing esthetic reflection to bear on the objects and practices of religion helps us to see them more clearly, to understand how they are like and different from other religious objects and actions, and identify the response they evoke in the body.

Art creates and comments on a world, and religious art creates and comments on a religious world. Paying close attention to the elements of narrative (e.g. character, narration, plot, and dialogue), visual composition (e.g. point of view, angle, editing, lighting, and color), and musical structure (e.g. meter, timbre, and rhythm) provides a clearer picture of the forms of these created worlds, their internal structures and logic. Attending to such aspects can be challenging for an observer in his or her first encounter with that world.

Developing the critical skills to identify and interpret its mediated forms deepens one's understanding of any faith tradition or new religious practice. Practitioners of religions with sacred writings have long meditated on these texts. Believers study the sacred writings, and the language and images from the texts move into practice, shaping private and public worship and serving as ethical and imaginative guides to life. They produce elaborate, visually beautiful versions of the texts, transforming them into sacred objects. Of course, not all mediations of religion are literary. The mediation of a religion might be graphic, as with the petroglyphs in the Teton Mountains of Wyoming that illustrate the spirit world of the ancient Shoshone (Figure 8.1), or the icons of saints looking down from the dome of a Greek Orthodox Church. The religious experience might be mediated aurally, as when the Muslim call to prayer resonates across Tehran, or when a Pentecostal seized by the Holy Spirit speaks in tongues. Think also of incense, the smell of yak butter lamps at a Tibetan monastery, and other smells that evoke particular religious responses, and embodied forms like dance, procession, and spirit possession that evoke the sacred. Understanding these forms of expression more clearly provides a vocabulary to describe religious experience.

Reading: texts and their ritual use

As discussed in earlier chapters, literacy changed religious communities in ways we probably do not fully understand. Stories, histories, and records that once existed as oral traditions were written down. When that happened they were codified, which meant that only particular versions of the traditions were legitimated and preserved. Writing became a space where religious ideas could be developed and contested. Authority once given to those who could

Figure 8.1 Petroglyphs

remember and recite now passed to those who could read and write. In many traditions particular texts came to be viewed as uniquely connecting the believer to the sacred. Thus, for over 150 years Protestant children, often before they can read, have been taught to sing "Jesus loves me! This I know, for the Bible tells me so" (Warner 1860). The hymn implies that faith in Jesus is not simply confirmed by experience but by the text that is sacred to Christian tradition. This power of the sacred text is so great that it is venerated even by believers who may not yet read. To understand religions where reading is so important we will want to know more about their texts.

Texts

Studying the form and content of the religious texts themselves deepens our understanding of the religion and the way participants relate to the texts. What are these texts about, how are they organized, and what literary forms and genres are used? As the Protestant children described above begin to read the Christian Bible, they will discover that it is a collection of writings containing a wide variety of different kinds of literature. There are histories, poems, stories, and laws. Different books of the Bible, and even sections of books, were written by different people at different times and often with unique concerns or agendas. Biblical scholar John Dominic Crossan suggests that some are myths that explain things like the origin of the world or the reasons for living piously. Some are apologies, stories that justify something such as the organization of society. At the other extreme, some are parables that attack the organization of society, pointing out and mocking its inconsistencies (1973). Recognizing these different literary forms allows the reader to read them in relationship to other material in the Bible, compare and contrast them to other stories in the cultures that produced them, and think about how these sacred stories are similar to and different from the sacred texts of other traditions. With this background the reader is more likely to notice particular patterns, characters, and events. For instance, recognizing a story as a parable cues the reader to watch for the element that would surprise and shock the original hearers of the story.

Of course, religion's mediation through reading and writing is not limited to sacred texts. The Protestant children described above will discover that their co-religionists write their faith in tracts and on Sunday School posters; they express it on billboards, bumper stickers, and in digital spaces. Representatives of many religions use printed texts to offer instruction manuals for the faithful; create religious stories, poems, and novels; write sometimes competing histories; debate interpretations of sacred texts; issue judgments on religious law; articulate theologies; and argue among themselves. They also write tracts for potential converts, letters to the editor, editorials, and press releases expressing their position on issues in society. They use writing for internal communication and to engage those outside their community. Attending to all of these practices expands our picture of mediated religion.

Much of modern education is focused on producing more sophisticated readers. Students start with fairly simple critical tasks, such as identifying the characters and actions in a story. They learn to put the narrative in order, identifying causality and chronology. They learn to analyze characters' motivation. Teachers urge their students to identify the conflict at the core of the story and to ask how it is resolved and how characters are changed by the resolution.

Studying literature encourages a reader to think in more complex ways about narratives, recognize a wider range of literary types, and put each story in its literary, historical, and cultural contexts. Cultural criticism teaches the reader to wonder how issues of power such as race, class, gender, and sexual orientation shape the context of the author, how she or he draws on or challenges the norms of the culture within which the story was written, and how these matters shape the perspective of the reader. Because sacred texts are first of all texts, subject to the same interpretive processes as other texts, developing skills as readers helps us understand and interpret the religious text, the religious tradition and culture in which it is practiced.

Ritual use of texts

How and where are sacred texts read? Are they more than simply the containers of information? Are they objects to be venerated? Are they displayed and handled in particular ways? Do particular people read them at particular times? Asking such questions can give us clues about the religions that are associated with each text.

Consider the way that modern Jews treat the Torah. The consecrated space of a synagogue includes an ark, an ornate cabinet, often with a curtain over it, which contains a Torah scroll. This copy of the Torah is not printed like a modern book; it is a beautiful scroll written in Hebrew that must be rolled out to the appropriate passage. At the appropriate time it is reverently taken out and carried to the *bema*, a raised platform from which it is read. These ritual spaces and actions proclaim the sacredness of the Torah, both the object and its message, and set a context for its reading. In the ritual of bar or bat mitzvah, during which an observant Jew becomes an adult member of the faith community, the honoree comes to the *bema* to read a passage from the Torah.

Other religions have ritual uses of their own sacred texts, some within the consecrated worship space and others in more public spaces. When an American football fan holds up a placard reading "John 3:16," the use of this verse from the New Testament is intended to bring the sacred content of the Christian scriptures into the profane public square and perhaps to lead readers to seek out the content of this passage.

Writing is also one way that religions critique each other, and religion itself is contested. As with any other subject, we can learn about religion by reading what its critics have to say about its ideas and rituals. One might read atheist Richard Dawkins's *The God Delusion* (2006), for instance, or an editorial in a Hindi newspaper about the actions and motivations of Buddhists in a region where members of the two traditions contest for political power and the control of sacred spaces. Considering the arguments of a religion's detractors not only sheds light on the particular religion but also on the religious worldview of the writer.

Reading as metaphor

Learning to read is a powerful experience that gives the new reader access to a wider world. Perhaps for this reason reading a written text serves as a common metaphor for what happens when people engage in other esthetic experiences. Therefore other mediations are sometimes called "texts" and the process of engaging with them referred to as "reading." Thus, the critical viewer might be described as "reading" a film and the critical listener as "reading" a song or symphony. The allusion to reading can be helpful in that it reminds us that apprehending is an act of interpretation. Yet this analogical thinking can be problematic when it leads us to reduce a film to its dialogue or a song to its lyrics.

Such a reduction imperfectly describes our esthetic experience. Watching a movie or hearing a piece of music requires attention to much more than the words. When religion and media scholars first began to study popular music, they tended to focus almost entirely on the lyrics. Doing so reduces the songs to narrative texts without attending to how musical form interacts with the words, which contributes to our experience of the piece as a whole. Music theory reminds the listener that the piece is more fully understood if we give attention to matters of musical form like rhythm, meter, and vocal quality and to the influence of musical genres like opera, gospel, pop, and hip hop.

The analogy to reading remains powerful because it reminds us that there are certain skills required to fully participate in an esthetic experience. In learning to read, almost everyone first struggles to recognize individual letters and then to assemble them into words and sentences and paragraphs. As readers become more adept they begin to recognize and understand narrative patterns, characters, and themes. By becoming more attentive readers they begin to make sense of new literary forms, deepening their appreciation of literature. A similar learning curve is necessary with the other arts through which religion might be mediated.

Listening: music, speech and silence

"Reading," in the metaphorical sense described just above also involves opening one's ears. Listening is a key skill for those who want to understand religion and religious experience. Listening is itself a religious discipline. When Sufis gather for the practice that they call *Sama* or "listening," they play music and dance ecstatically. They explain that dancing opens them to the divine music, whose source is the deity. Jews and Christians cite the story of the Prophet Elijah (I Kings 11–13), who experiences the Holy One of Israel not in great wind, earthquake, or fire, but in a "still small voice." For these practitioners, listening is a way to experience the sacred, to be open to the presence of deity.

When we listen to religion, we seek to identify the sounds, the speech acts, and the silences that are part of a particular religious ritual, experience, or tradition. Attending to aural expression of religion raises questions about religious practice. What might the clear, high-pitched tone of the Tibetan *tingsha* bell tell us about Buddhist meditation? Does the sheer volume of a Pentecostal worship service blasting from the speakers on the roof of a Guatemalan chapel express something about the Pentecostal Christians' understanding of the actions of the Holy Spirit or illuminate their relationship to their neighbors? What do the *sumbel*, or toasts, offered to the gods and the ancestors by Neopagan practitioners of the Old Norse religion of *Ásatrú* reveal about their hopes and concerns?

Music

Learning to hear and appreciate music sharpens the listening skills and provides a vocabulary to describe more clearly the form and patterns of the sounds of religion (Figure 8.2). Though not all these sounds are musical, attention to rhythm, melody, and harmony trains the listener to experience the sound of religion in its complexity. In *What to Listen for in Music* (2009) composer Aaron Copland (1937–2009) suggests that three things are going on at once when we listen to music. First we experience music on what he calls the "sensuous plane." This is our pure sensual appreciation of the music itself, before we have applied higher-order critical thinking to it. Next is the "expressive plane." Here our pleasure in the piece of music is related to its evocation of something outside the music, perhaps an emotion like happiness, anger, or sexual arousal; perhaps a sense of space, as the raging of a storm or the waves of the sea; perhaps a feeling such as patriotism or devotion. Copland says that it is on this plane that a piece of music is said to mean something. Finally, the composer

Figure 8.2 Pre-school choir

informs us, the piece functions on a "musical plane," that of "the notes themselves and of their manipulation" (Copland 2009: 21). On this third plane musical patterns are being developed and musical problems solved. Take the familiar "Hallelujah Chorus" from George Frideric Handel's *Messiah*. On the first plane, listeners simply experience the majestic music rolling over them. Though the piece contains words, it is the soaring sound of the choir that takes center stage. On the second plane, the piece evokes a sense of triumphal accomplishment for many listeners. The music itself, the words of the chorus, and perhaps the listeners' knowledge of the history of the piece may evoke Christ's resurrection, even in a secular concert hall. At the same time, musically trained listeners are attuned to the third plane, aware of how the Chorus resolves musical patterns and antecedents established earlier in the piece.

While there are religious experiences that do not involve music, and even some religions that ban all or some forms of music, for the most part when religious communities gather, music is involved. In addition to the examples noted above, think of the drumming and singing that accompany the Sun Dance of the First Nations of North America, the throat singing of animistic Tuvan people of southern Siberia, or the *kagura* performed to entertain the gods at Shinto shrines in Japan. The combination of music and ritual is used in a similar way in civil ceremonies like the opening of the Olympics, memorial gatherings honoring the war dead or the inauguration of national leaders in order to lend a sense of the sacred to these enterprises.

Certainly, music is not the only sound of religion. The tramp of feet in procession, the sound of water poured out in baptism, and the murmur of prayers are each part of the sound of religion at work. As with religious texts, these sounds are not limited to the formal ritual spaces of religion; practitioners carry them into other spaces of their lives. At Nashville's Grand Ole Opry the country songs of hard work and lost love are interspersed with Southern gospel music. The names of deities are invoked in unexpected places for both sacred and profane purposes. One can hear Buddhist prayer flags flap in the wind outside both houses in Lhasa, Tibet, and dorm rooms in San Francisco, California.

Speech

A central sound of religion is that of human speech. In a range of traditions the ritual includes some combination of songs sung, sacred texts read aloud, prayers uttered, liturgies chanted, excommunications pronounced, stories from the tradition told, sermons or other proclamations made aloud, and periods of silence. In the Seder ritual a young Jew asks, "Why is this night different from all other nights?" A Zen master lays out a koan, asking the initiate, "What is the sound of one hand clapping?" At an American Thanksgiving dinner, each guest is often asked to name something for which she or he is thankful. Speech, like music, is aural—made up of sounds that fall upon the ear. It can give sensual pleasure or grate on the ear, regardless of the content of the words that comprise it. Though usually less formally so than music, speech is patterned, and we owe our satisfaction as listeners in part to the way the words are both organized and vocalized. If the text of Rev. Martin Luther King, Jr.'s "I Have a Dream" speech were reproduced here, many readers would find it a moving call for racial justice. But the full power of the speech is inseparable from the cadences of King's voice, his rhythms and repetitions of language. Just as Copland reminds us that there is a purely musical plane in the appreciation of music, there is a plane of the pure sound of speech. Consider the fact that the spoken delivery of a message is called a "speech;" this word emphasizes that listeners to a speech are invited to hear not only the content but also the way the words are spoken. Hearing a speech rather than just reading the text provides access to the cadences of delivery and the modulations of the voice, and thus gives greater access to the emotional impact of the words on those who first heard them spoken.

Silence

There is much sound in religion, but silence is also important. One of the patterns within the sounds of religion is the periods of reflective silence. In the monastic traditions in Buddhism, Christianity, and Hinduism, people may commit themselves to lives of silent reflection. For others silence is a more intermittent practice, with silent retreats, periods of meditation, or times of silence during worship services to invite private prayer or reflection. In fact, the travel section of the *Wall Street Journal* reports that the silent retreat has become a part of the commodification of religion, with monasteries and retreat centers marketing to persons of any or no religious tradition as a form of vacation from the busyness of modern life (*WSJ*, September 7, 2012).

Watching

Much of the mediation of religion is visual. From the ancient Egyptians' Great Sphinx of Giza, to Katsina dolls of the Pueblo people, to the Buddhist prayer tattooed on the back of movie star Angelina Jolie, religion is found in images and objects that invite the gaze. In medieval times cathedrals rose above European towns, making a visual statement about the dominance of the Christian God and the spread of Christendom. Biblical images along with pictures of the saints and martyrs are a central theme of European art history and are reproduced in sundry places such as Sunday school illustrations and refrigerator magnets. Similarly, the panoply of Hindu gods can be seen throughout Southeast Asia on images and statues in temples and museums but also painted on buses and placed on home altars.

There is theatricality to religious rituals, they involve performance, the manipulation of objects and spaces, and sometimes great spectacle. This is particularly evident in mass events: the sight of tens of thousands of Hindus gathering to bathe in the Ganges River in order to attain spiritual cleansing, of white-robed Candomblé practitioners joining the brightly dressed participants in the streets during Rio de Janeiro's Carnival, or of crowds gathering in Vatican Square in March of 2013 to await the smoke that would announce the election of Pope Francis paints religion large upon the landscape. There is theatricality in much smaller rituals as well. Practitioners express religious faith and identity when they gather and watch worship services or festivals, religious television, or other media, and they recognize their co-religionists by their actions and the symbols they display in such events. Whether or not students of religion and other observers share these people's faith they participate in a religious practice, if only as observers, when they watch a merchant burn incense before an image of the Buddha in her shop, read a bumper sticker announcing "Real men love Jesus," or see an Elvis Presley fan tenderly hanging a picture of the performer in his home.

Recognizing this visual quality in religion, it behooves those who want to understand religion to pay attention to its visual spectacle. Much of religion's mediation is constructed through visual images or moving pictures, and learning about the history and construction of the visual arts and film will enrich our understanding of religion. To engage such mediations one must consider what sort of religious world is being made visible.

Movies, like paintings, have a frame and the film-maker or painter includes some things, and excludes others from within the frame. This simple insight reminds the viewer that the image is contrived, that it reflects esthetic and sometimes political and theological choices. A film-maker, photographer, or painter chooses what to include within the frame, and thus what to exclude. Reflecting on this encourages a critical viewer of religions to ask what is included and excluded, and who has the authority to make these decisions. Learning to reflect on a painting or a film teaches one to consider the composition of the image, what do we see, and how is it arranged? Who dominates the image and who is pushed to the edge or recedes into the background? How are color and lighting used to encourage particular interpretations of what we see? How are these images, and stories they illumine, like and different from others?

Art, like religious practice, happens within or in reaction to a tradition. Pier Paulo Pasolini, the director of *The Gospel According to Saint Matthew* (1964), for instance, was influenced by the neo-realist style that developed in Italy following World War II. Italian film directors went out into the streets and countryside selecting their untrained actors for the visual quality of their faces and bodies rather than their acting skills. Understanding the neo-realist movement of film making helps put the look of *The Gospel According to Saint Matthew* in context and invites the viewer to think about how Pasolini uses the stark hillsides and ancient Italian villages to stand in for biblical spaces and to think of the actors themselves as a sort of visual landscape through which he tells the story.

Considering a religious ritual as a visual event encourages the viewer to see it clearly, to ponder its juxtapositions and movements. Once, while traveling in a remote region of Guatemala, I visited a stone church in the colonial style. At the front before an altar several Catholic priests said the mass in Spanish. Toward the back, directly down the central aisle Mayan priests carried out their traditional rituals in Quichean. Between them a handful of worshipers appeared to be caught visually, religiously, and culturally between two traditions. At first glance the two groups of priests seemed to compete for the attention and loyalty of the peasant worshipers. The Catholic priests occupied the front, and of course the church was arranged to focus the viewer on their actions. So a conventional visual interpretation suggests that the indigenous priests are usurpers in an alien space. But, picturing the worshipers as the center of this image alters my perspective on this event. They gave no visual evidence of choosing sides or shifting focus. Perhaps what I was seeing was not two competing rituals but one more complex ritualization of the religion of the region. If so, then something more complex than religious conflict is mediated in that space, and considering what it looked like is crucial to understanding how religion and religious identities were being constructed there.

Participating—attention to our bodily reactions

My experience in the Guatemalan sanctuary that seemed sacred to some combination of Catholic and Mayan sensibilities serves as reminder that our interactions with religion whether in physical or digital space are embodied. Whether we enter into them as practitioners, students of religion, or tourists, they evoke our own bodily sensations. Recalling that particular religiously complex space, the ritual and the people involved, evokes my bodily memory of the smells of bodies and incense, the brutal heat of the sun baking the high wooden roof and drifting through open doorways, the smoke of the fire that the Mayan priests tended drifting in the shaded sanctuary, the jostle of other bodies in the space, the imagined taste of the host and other sacrifices, and the sight of the gathered worshipers and the priests at work.

When bathing in the Ganges, Sufi dancing, drinking communion wine, and in many other acts, religion is mediated through the body. Whether people engage with mediations of religion on the page of ancient texts, in a sacred space, on a movie screen, or in a digital location, they do not leave their bodies behind. In digital space our human sensate response may depend more on the eye and the ear, but the body responds, our pulse may calm or quicken, we may be attracted, interested, or bored. Developing the esthetic skills of reading, listening, and watching helps the practitioner to more fully experience the tradition and assists the observer in describing and interpreting them in ways that "flesh out" one's understanding of religious practices. Interpretations are rooted not only in theory but in bodily sensation.

Discussion questions

1   What training have you had in studying arts such as literature, visual art, film, music, or architecture? How might you draw on this training in studying religion and media?

2   Describe a religious event (a worship service, a pilgrimage, a mourning site, etc.) that you have observed or participated in as an esthetic experience. How is the space organized? What sounds, smells, and sights guide the participants' experience of the sacred? What are people doing with their bodies? What do we learn about the particular event, the tradition, and/or religion in general by paying attention to these things?

3   An esthetic approach trains us to pay attention to patterns and genres. It asks how is this particular experience like, and different from, other seemingly similar experiences. Read a religious text, listen to a piece of sacred music, or continue to think about the religious event you considered in the previous question. What esthetic patterns do you observe? What do they contribute to the experience?

4   Attention to esthetics makes us aware of how a painter or film-maker directs the viewers' attention by framing, composition, and lighting and how a storyteller shapes the tale and controls the available information to produce particular effects. Are religious experiences similarly staged to produce particular spiritual effects?

5   What are the implications of thinking of religion as an esthetic, sensual, and bodily experience? What does an esthetic approach to the study of religion and media add to our understandings of the mediation of religion?

6. In the reflections that follow, Clanton discusses how the musical elements and lyrics in a Katy Perry video come together, while Plate thinks about how a particular camera movement has similar meaning in a variety of quite different films. Both suggest that these secular popular entertainments draw on religious concepts that are communicated esthetically. Does such an analysis give you a richer experience of video and films? Why, or why not? What does it suggest about the way the religious is present in seemingly secular culture?

References

Copland, Aaron (2009) *What to Listen for in Music*, New York: New American Library, a division of Penguin Group (USA), Inc.

Crossan, John Dominic (1973) *In Parables: The Challenge of the Historical Jesus*, New York: Harper and Row.

Dawkins, Richard (2006) *The God Delusion*, Boston: Houghton Mifflin.

Wall Street Journal (WSJ) (2012) "Don't Say a Word," September 7.

Warner, Susan (1860) *Jesus Loves Me*, #191 in the 1989 edition of *The United Methodist Hymnal*, Nashville: The United Methodist Publishing House.

Reflection
Creating mythology through cinematography

S. Brent Plate

Movie after movie begins the same way: In the beginning is the extreme long shot of the sky above, then the camera tilts down to the social order here below. Each shot progressively creates a tighter and tighter frame until we zoom in on the main characters who are involved in some sort of conflict: human vs. human, human vs. alien, human vs. self.

Hundreds of movies have begun with a similar structure, but here we will compare the first few shots of three totally different productions: the science fiction *Star Wars: Episode IV* (dir. George Lucas, 1977), the surrealistic suspense *Blue Velvet* (dir. David Lynch, 1986), and the dark comedy *Bad Santa* (dir. Terry Zwigoff, 2003). None of these is a "religious film" per se, but each uses cinematography to create a narrative that is akin to the mythologizing process at the heart of religious practice. To get into the deep structures of film-making is to find surprising parallels to the deep structures of religious traditions.

At first, the universe appears in proper working order when looked at from far away. "God's in his heaven—All's right with the world!" said poet Robert Browning (1947), and cinematographers delight in a God's eye view of things. In their opening shots, *Blue Velvet* offers up a clear blue day, while *Star Wars* and *Bad Santa* give us the starry firmament.

Then the camera tilts down, and the shots that follow offer an image of the *nomos*, the social order "here below" on earth that mirrors the cosmic order "up above." The second, third, and fourth shots in *Blue Velvet* bring us into a small town neighborhood with picket fences, friendly firemen, and crossing guards (Figure 8.3). The camera in *Bad Santa* brings us to the interior space of O'Hara's Pub, a nicely appointed bar with well-dressed, smiling people drinking white wine. *Star Wars* does not change shots so much as offers the scrolling "prologue" which tells of the way things are going in the world that we the viewers are about to enter.

Then comes the transition point, when the ordered cosmos and nomos give way to something not quite right, some sense of chaos lurking below the exteriors. *Blue Velvet*'s friction is marked by the appearance of a gun on television, and the rattling water spigot of a man irrigating his lawn. *Bad Santa* closes in on a sad-looking man (Billy Bob Thornton) in a Santa

Figure 8.3 Blue Velvet opening shot

suit at the end of the bar; he gives a drunken, profanity-laden voiceover narration as he stares into a mirror smoking a cigarette. *Star Wars* evokes chaos as the camera finishes tilting down, the high-percussion music swells, and ultimately two spacecraft are engaged in a laser-shooting battle—and then we go inside a ship to find the troubled Princess Leia.

The conflict is cemented as the depths of troubles of the characters are revealed: The man in *Blue Velvet* has a stroke and falls to the ground; "Santa" is seen vomiting in an alley outside the bar, Santa suit still intact; Princess Leia is captured by the ominous Darth Vader.

The same framing narrative is achieved in creation mythologies around the world, for example, in the first three chapters of Genesis. The biblical book's first view is large, showing the expanses of the universe, which slowly builds toward the earth, other creatures, and finally to the protagonists: Adam and Eve, at which point conflict also ensues.

And so the stories begin: cosmos leads to nomos, leads to chaos, leads to the ongoing battle between these realms. Myths, like films, utilize well-worn patterns of production, with the ultimate purpose of bringing the audience into the world of the narrative. Always similar enough to be familiar, but different enough to be new and enticing: whether long ago and far away space travelers, or a drunken department store Santa, or a naked couple in a garden.

Reference

Browning, Robert (1947) *Pippa Passes and Shorter Poems*, New York: The Odyssey Press.

Reflection
Katy Perry's *Firework*
Dan Clanton

Katy Perry's number one hit *Firework* draws on a familiar religious image, that of light. However, few listeners have paid close attention to the religious symbolism and the biblical subtext in the song's lyrics and accompanying video. While one does not have to engage the religious symbolism inherent in the song or its video, doing so allows one to place the song and its appeal in a broader context, perhaps alongside other songs such as the civil rights anthem, *This Little Light of Mine*. Doing so helps us see how the pop song makes an ethical claim and involves an evangelical invitation to the light.

Figure 8.4 Katy Perry

Perry tells her listener—whom she assumes has feelings of isolation and inadequacy—that "there's a spark in you," and once they "ignite the light and let it shine," that "like a lightning bolt, your heart will glow." This internal light is "even brighter than the moon," and "now it's time to let it through." The point of the lyrics seems clear: Perry is encouraging her listeners to find strength and courage in themselves in order to not be afraid to be who they are, to live their lives proudly and confidently. The song's dance-hall beat, anthemic nature, and catchy chorus complement the empowering lyrics, and encourage listeners to interact with it, either through sound or movement. Musically, the ascending tones and crescendo in the chorus, as well as the major key signature, lead the listener to Perry's central affirmation, that the listener is a *Firework* and, as such, the musical complements the lyrical. The video of the song accentuates this reading of the lyrics, as the viewer is shown images of emotionally abused children, a young woman ashamed of her body, a young cancer patient, and a young gay man. These brief scenes are interspersed with scenes of Perry singing while flashes of light and fireworks shoot forth from her chest. Seeing these allows the other characters to act in order to resolve or improve their situations, and the video concludes with a crowd of people dancing, many of whom have fireworks shooting from them as well.

This imagery of light is used in a similar way in both Jewish and Christian thought. In Genesis 1.3, God commands there to be light, yet this is neither the sun nor the stars. Some Jewish scriptural interpreters hold this light to be the "splendor of the divine presence," and others see this light as representing the spark of divinity that is present in each human, which longs to be returned to God through the performance of moral and ethical commandments. Similarly, in the Christian tradition light plays a key role. In Jesus' Sermon on the Mount, he tells his hearers that "You are the light of the world," and admonishes them to "Let your light shine before others, so that they may see your good works" (Matthew 5.14–16). The Gospel of John claims that in Jesus there is life, "and the life was the light of all people. The light shines in the darkness, and the darkness did not overcome it" (1.4–5). Based on these Gospels, theologians have encouraged Christians to engage in ethical decision making and moral action based on their belief in Jesus. In *Firework*, Perry, whether consciously or not, draws on this religious sense that light expresses promise and invites ethical choice.

9   Case studies

Below, three concrete examples of the interface of media, religion, and culture that were referenced in earlier chapters are described more fully. They come from different cultural and religious locations and involve different mediations of religion. Each is followed by reflection questions to invite the reader's analysis.

Jyllands-Posten cartoons of Muhammad

On September 30, 2005, the Danish newspaper *Jyllands-Posten* published a dozen editorial cartoons depicting the Prophet Muhammad. The cartoons are not reproduced here, but those who wish to view them can find them on the Web with English translations. The paper's editors gave two reasons for publishing the cartoons. They described them as an effort to catalyze a debate about Islam following several highly publicized acts of international terrorism by Islamic extremists, and to challenge what they understood to be self-censorship in the Nordic press in response to Muslim sensibilities.

Many Danish Muslims took deep offense at the cartoons (Figure 9.1). Islam, particularly its Sunni branch, opposes representations of the human form of its revered prophet. Mocking or insulting the Prophet is deemed blasphemy and is religiously prohibited by Muslims. In countries from which many Muslim immigrants came, blasphemy is a punishable civil offense. Critics of the cartoons argued that they were insensitive and reflected a racist and religiously intolerant double standard. Supporters of the publication responded that freedom of speech was a critical principle whether or not one agreed with the particular statements in the cartoons. Further, some argued, it was useful for both secular and religious Danes to discuss the place of Islam in Danish society.

Those opposed to the cartoons replied that appeals to free speech were applied inconsistently: Danish Christians were not subjected to similar use of their holy symbols and figures by the press, and the commitment to free speech was used to justify an Islamophobic response intended to humiliate a religious and cultural minority.

For a period, it appeared that the controversy would pass relatively benignly. But imams in Denmark appealed to the Danish government to do more than

Figure 9.1 Protest march against the depictions of Muhammad in a Danish newspaper

reiterate the Danish commitment to free speech. They also petitioned Muslim nations to address the offense. By early 2006 the cartoons, and the charges of the Danish Muslim protesters, had become widely known in the Islamic world, leading to campaigns to boycott Danish goods, death threats, riots, attacks on Danish and other Western institutions, and ultimately to the deaths of several hundred people.

Discussion questions

1 In the cartoons Islam is mediated in images created from outside the Muslim community. Who do you think can best interpret a religion? What kind of power or authority do insiders who participate in the religion and outside observers have in describing and interpreting religious practice and belief? Are there special skills required to interpret religion? Are objective descriptions possible? What is the role of the press and of scholars in developing public understandings of religion and its place in society? Should religion have special protections from potentially hurtful or inaccurate outsider interpretations? Should the press treat religion differently from other topics?
2 What understandings of the freedom and responsibility of the press are at work in the decision of the *Jyllands-Posten* editors to print the cartoons and in the responses of the critics and defenders?
3 How do the competing values of secularity and freedom of religious expression play out in this situation? Do these tensions exist in your country, and how are they understood and balanced?

4 Why do you think that the responses in predominantly Muslim countries were so strong? What does the controversy reveal about religion and its struggle with modernity?

Pentecostal films in Ghana and Nigeria

In Ghana and Nigeria a new media culture emerged in the early 1990s when cheap video technologies converged with democratization to relax the government's control of the mass media. A local movie industry emerged, producing low-budget melodramatic features about Africans and African concerns. *The New York Times Magazine* reported, "Most of the movies themselves are awful, marred by slapdash production, melodramatic acting and ludicrous plots" (Rice 2012: paragraph 4). Yet the article asserts that the movies are so popular that this industry produces more films than Hollywood, ranking second in the world in the sheer number of movies produced only to India's thriving Bollywood industry (Figure 9.2).

Ethnographer Birgit Meyer, who has extensively studied this media culture, says that Pentecostals produce and vigorously market melodramas rooted in an African charismatic religious worldview. According to Meyer, the films' Pentecostalism and the use of the English language cut across traditional ethnic divisions, which serves to unify the audience. The movies play in local theaters and, distributed on cheap video CDs, act as a religious and cultural link for a large expatriate audience in Europe and North America (Meyer 2003).

Typical plots of these films focus on problems within the family or workplace and on the trials of Pentecostal believers. In the Pentecostal worldview common to the region, the Devil and his minions are powerful forces engaged in a spiritual war with God and God's angels. The low-budget video

Figure 9.2 Film market in Lagos

productions present this warfare as a visual reality, often portraying those who practice traditional African religions as the servants of the evil forces.

One example, *Attacks from Home* (n.d., written, directed and produced by Mike Bamiloye), tells of conflicts in the London office of a Nigerian business. Pentecostal employees gather at lunchtime and after work to pray for the good of the company as well as for their more personal concerns until a non-believing manager forbids them to practice at the office. Things are compounded when an employee at home in Lagos, desiring the post of the manager in London, turns to a traditional witch doctor for help in securing the position. The witch doctor's practices call forth dark forces and bring about the death of the London rival. The Lagos employee moves to the London office, which launches an elaborate spiritual conflict. In the end, the Pentecostals and their God triumph after many trials.

Meyer suggests that the audience and the film-makers understand that the spirit appearances and traditional rituals portrayed in the films, and the rituals and material that call them forth, are tricks of video editing and composition. Nonetheless she reports that many viewers, actors, and producers take them as the portrayal of actual spiritual forces. According to Meyer, the producers regard the portrayal of these dark forces as itself fraught with spiritual danger, for they believe that disembodied evil spirits are abroad in the world looking for material spaces and persons which they might inhabit. For the producers and their intended audience the movies are more than illustration, they are a location of this spiritual warfare. Meyer writes that the video camera is "engaged in a new way of mediating Jesus ... and creating a new form of public religiosity hovering around a camera-derived mystification" (Meyer 2003: 3).

Discussion questions

1 If *The New York Times Magazine* article is correct and these movies are generally "awful, marred by slapdash production, melodramatic acting and ludicrous plots," then why are the movies so popular? What does this tell you about the relationship of media and religion?

2 What do the films reveal about how religion responds to changes in media culture? How does religion seem to have changed in Ghana and Nigeria, and how has the changing media context contributed to that change? What does the absence of Christian clergy in *Attacks from Home* suggest about how these African Pentecostals think about religious authority and access to the sacred? What is the location and focus of a religious life, as portrayed in these films?

3 How does Pentecostalism both resist and align itself with modernity in these films?

4 Consider how traditional African religions are depicted in these films. What does it imply about the tension between traditional religions and Christianity that is taking place in some African countries? Is the medium of film an effective location for that contest?

PostSecret

"PostSecret is an ongoing community art project where people mail in their secrets anonymously on one side of a homemade postcard," reads an explanation at www.postsecret.com. Every Sunday the webmasters of PostSecret post photos of a selection of these mysterious submissions. The site shows that, as of August 2013, nearly 627 million viewers have visited it, and scores also follow it on Facebook. Archival postcards can be seen online and in PostSecret books. Some followers gather in small face-to-face groups to view and discuss the posts on a weekly basis, and the founder of PostSecret, Frank Warren, appears at public events, often on college campuses, to discuss his compelling creation.

Some PostSecret cards are homemade or modified by the submitter; others are premade postcards or notecards, and the creativity of the submitter lies in the juxtaposition of the card and the message written on it. The secrets include hidden desires, reflections on the writer's body or character, reports of sexual transgressions, criminal activities, embarrassing moments, regrets, and expressions of religious faith or doubt. Though some seem merely playful or boastful, many have a confessional quality. Perhaps submitters hope that in their anonymous sharing they will be unburdened and experience a sense of forgiveness or release (Figure 9.3).

In his book on the multimedia phenomenon of PostSecret, founder Frank Warren writes that participating is healing for those who send submissions to

Figure 9.3 PostSecret project

PostSecret and inspiring for those who follow it. He feels it creates an anonymous community of acceptance (Warren 2007). Visitors may come to the website as often as they want to peruse the sometimes troubling, sometimes beautiful cards.

Among the posts on www.postsecret.com in the first week of August 2013 were the following:

- A Georgia lottery ticket marked with the words "I play with the hope of being able to afford medication and therapy."
- A photo of light falling across a plaster wall inscribed with "I have been volunteering at the hospice for the last year hoping that, out of necessity, I will learn to believe in God."
- A Victorian image of a young girl covered with hearts and the comment "I corrected his grammar in bed."
- A death certificate from a suicide with "I forgive you Dad" scrawled across the edge.
- A reproduction of a female nude by Renoir with "He likes my curves— a lot."
- A page from a mathematics text headed "Like and Unlike Terms" modified by the phrase "I wish living a Christian life was as straightforward as math equations."
- A picture of two dogs nuzzling through a fence along with the words "When I told them I was gay my ultra-religious brother—stopped letting me spend time alone with my nieces and nephews—ironically he sexually abused me when we were growing up."

Discussion questions

1 The creator of PostSecret describes it as an "ongoing community art project." In what ways is this "art?" What does it reveal about the formation and expression of identity in digital space? How is it connected to changing understandings of community and authority?

2 What is the role of confession in religion, and what is the importance of confessing to the person wronged, to a priest or another religious leader, or to God? Does sending a submission to PostSecret serve some or all of the religious functions of confession?

3 Apart from the idea of confession, is there a ritual or religious quality to the process of submitting to or following PostSecret? What is gained or lost by describing this as a religious activity?

4 Can religion exist in online spaces like PostSecret? How does the online location contribute to, or detract from, the PostSecret experience?

References

Meyer, Birgit (2003) "Impossible Representations, Pentecostalism, Vision and Video Technology in Ghana," Working Paper No. 25, Institut für Ethnologie und Afrikastudien, Johannes Gutenberg-Universität, Forum 6, D-55099 Mainz, Germany.

Rice, Andrew (2012) "A Scorsese in Lagos: The Making of Nigeria's Film Industry," *New York Times Magazine*, February 23.

Warren, Frank (2007) *My Secret: A PostSecret Book*, London: Orion Books.

Glossary of key terms

Below, some key terms used in *Media, Religion and Culture: An Introduction* are briefly defined in the context of the way they are used here and in the broader discourse about media, religion, and culture. Many of these terms are discussed more fully in the body of this volume, and their definitions are debated by scholars who attempt to use them with precision.

Belief A *belief* is a conviction about something not necessarily subject to vigorous proof, such as a belief in the existence of God, or other spiritual beings, forces, or powers. The term also often refers to particular religious tenets or doctrines, as in the phrase "Christian beliefs." See the contrast to *practice*.

Civil religion This term refers to rituals, language, and attitudes which treat the nation and its principles as sacred. *Civil religion* refers to all ritual venerations of the state, its leaders, and honored dead, especially, but not exclusively, when overtly religious language is used.

Consumption The idea of *consumption* first points to any process of acquiring and disposing of goods. It is used here more narrowly to suggest that today some people acquire religious images and objects, such as a statue of the Hindu goddess Kali or an ornate Christian crucifix, in ways that are disconnected from their location in systems of belief and practice, and use them as esthetic expressions of individual identity. Consumption is also evident when people "shop" for a religious community that meets their personal needs, or when they treat the spiritual material and practices of others more generally as something they can acquire and repurpose.

Culture Everything that human beings make and maintain through language, ritual activity, and construction (art, architecture, technologies, etc.) can be thought of as part of *culture*. A specific culture is a project of shared identity construction that establishes boundaries that include some people and exclude others, as in the phrase "the culture of Eastern Europe".

Digital What is known as new media today is made possible by technologies that allow the *digital* division of images and information into bits which can be modified and/or reorganized by computers. This ability to sample and appropriate information in new ways becomes a metaphor for the way that individual identity and culture is created in the digital age.

Function The concept of social *function* provides a way to talk about religion and other social practices apart from the self-understanding of the participants. The functionalist asks what work a practice, image, or object does for the individual, community, or wider society. Thus a group of teens with a Ouija Board might say that it provides guidance from the spiritual world about life choices, while the functionalist might suggest that this practice provides assurance about the reliability of the world in the face of adolescent anxiety.

Hyphenation The idea of *hyphenation* is borrowed from written construction. Two concepts like action and reflection are linked with a hyphen (action-reflection) to signal that they are linked parts of a larger process. It is used here to think about the way that people locate their religious practice simultaneously in two communities of belief and practice such as the Hindu-Christian or the Jew-Bu(ddhist).

Late-modernity The concept of *late-modernity* suggests an era in which people have begun to doubt the tenets of modernity. While many of the social structures of modernity remain, people lack faith that modernity leads to progress and consensus, and thus the term implies that modernity must soon be replaced by some new cultural epoch. See also *modernity* and *postmodernity*.

Media The plural of medium is *media*, the various forms of communication. Colloquially, media is used to refer collectively to the news and/or entertainment industries.

Media culture The term *media culture* refers to the way that human societies are organized around and by the media of their day, whether it is cave paintings, writing, or Twitter. The term points to the unique cultural and religious expressions that develop in response to the media available, making possible new understandings of what it means to be human. A media revolution might be said to take place when new media disrupt and reshape a media culture.

Media space People create real-time visual and audio environments, interact socially, work, and create together in digital environments. The term *media space* serves as a reminder that such media serve as locations of human community and interaction. The concept counters the sense of media as simple depositories or delivery systems for information.

Mediate *Mediate* is the verb form of media; it points to the way that communication technologies, language, and practices communicate ideas or experiences. But the concept refers to more than simply the transfer of information, it calls attention to the way the idea or experience is shaped by the form of its expression.

Medium Any form through which human beings communicate can be described as a *medium*. Examples include language, touch, and movement, as well as the tools of amplification and articulation such as writing, visual image, music, film and video, and various digital forms of communication.

Modernity *Modernity* is the period in which a series of post-medieval movements came together. They include the development of the nation-state, capitalism, science, and the development of the Enlightenment ideals of reason, the modern individual, and the individual conscience. Key among modernity's tenets is confidence in the ability of reason and science to resolve all questions. Modernity implies not only these social changes but the belief that modernity leads to progress and agreement among people. See the contrasts to *late-modernity* and *postmodernity*.

Network A *network* is a relationship established between multiple overlapping groups. Rather than identity being tied to a single primary community or social location, it is established in these often shifting connections. In thinking about religion, the term is used to point to a shift away from religious identity tied to a single institutionalized community to identity articulated through the integration of multiple sources and communities.

New media While any emerging communications technology might be a *new* medium, *new media* refers to the development of digital media. The term particularly points to the way that digital media allows the sampling and assembly of fragments of information and to the interactivity that invites response and conversation.

Para-religion The concept of *para-religion* is used by those who wish to make a distinction between religion itself and things that seem similar to religion, and which serve some of the functions of religion, but which it is argued are not religion.

Postmodernity As modernity came to be seen as a Western invention, and as increased exposure to other cultures led people to question whether universal "truths" existed, people began to imagine a *post-modern* era characterized by suspicion of the assumptions of the modern period, one with greater openness to differing and irresolvable understandings of reality. See also *modernity* and *late-modernity*.

Practice In contrast to *belief*, the idea of religious *practice* suggests that religion is most helpfully described by focusing on the things that adherents actually do.

Religion A working definition of *religion* includes the various ways in which human beings and their communities relate to the sacred, including their beliefs and practices and the way they have created institutions to organize and contain the sacred.

Ritual A *ritual* is a practice that through its symbols and repetition expresses a connection to the sacred, or to other shared values and commitments.

Thus, among religious Jews eating the Seder meal recalls the acts of God in leading their fore-parents out of captivity, and among patriotic British citizens singing *God Save the Queen* venerates the Queen as a symbol of the state, its values, and traditions.

Sampling The term *sampling* comes from the world of hip hop, in which DJs extract fragments of larger musical recordings and juxtapose them against other fragments, which may be new or themselves sampled, in order to comment on them in new esthetic compositions. It is used here to point to the way that new media allow this process and to the way it becomes a part of identity construction within digital cultures.

Secularization *Secularization* is a social process that sees the public sphere as one free of sectarian distinction and protected from the distinctive claims of religion. In this process religion is privatized and, without the support of social systems, may become less common.

Shrine A *shrine* is a location where some image, relic, or other object is venerated in order to evoke a connection to the sacred. Shrines can be found within formal religious buildings, and in homes or public spaces. The term is often extended to seemingly secular sites so that Graceland, the home of Elvis, is described as a shrine to the singer.

Spiritual A concern for matters of the human soul or spirit is often described as *spiritual*. In contemporary usage the spiritual is often contrasted to religion, as in the phrase "spiritual but not religious." This usage implies an individualized spiritual life which may draw on the beliefs and practices of religion without being bound by religious institutions or authorities.

Symbol A *symbol* is a word, image or object which refers to something beyond itself, often to the sacred or to some concept, belief, or invisible reality. What makes the Christian cross a symbol is the fact that it does more than serve as a reminder of Jesus' suffering and death. For Christian believers it evokes Jesus' resurrection, and the interpretations of what his dying and rising mean in Christian thought.

Third spaces Sociology makes a distinction between purely public spaces, where all members of society can theoretically interact, and private spaces like the home or the ethnic social club. The concept of third spaces emerged to describe places like the coffee house that were neither fully public nor entirely private where people meet and engage one another. In thinking about digital culture it has been suggested that there are similar *third spaces* online that expand these in-between opportunities for informal social interaction.

Tradition *Tradition* is used in two ways in this volume. Sometimes it refers to a particular religious body with shared practices and beliefs that have continuity with the past. Thus one might be part of the Buddhist or

Wiccan tradition, or of a particular body within a broader religious community such as the Anglican tradition within Christianity. *Tradition* is also used to refer to other kinds of inherited social practice and understanding such as, for instance, the practice of making New Year's resolutions or kissing the Blarney Stone.

Transcoding The concept of *transcoding* is used to describe the ability to translate digital information from one format to another. Thus, a fragment from the recording of a speech that a politician makes before a particular audience might be posted on Facebook, included in a political fund-raising request, or juxtaposed against quite different things that the politician has said in other settings.

Annotated bibliography

There is an already extensive body of literature engaging the complex relationships and overlaps of media, religion, and culture. A literature search will reveal a cottage industry of journal articles, sole-authored books and anthologies reflecting a range of methods and field perspectives. A much longer critical bibliography could be offered, and in fact some can be found on the Internet. But no list is complete, raising questions of where to stop. And readers new to the field will likely find a shorter, selective list more helpful. Below 15 essays or book chapters are suggested. They represent something of the range of the conversation, and have been useful to others attempting to deepen and clarify the discourse about religion and/in its mediations.

The distinction between theoretical explorations and case studies is somewhat arbitrary. All the "theoretical" essays reflect on actual phenomena, if to varying degrees. In the "case studies," theoretically provocative examples invite broader reflections. The distinction points primarily to the fact that the case study essays let theory emerge out of conversation with and about a particular mediation of religion, while the theoretical essays draw on a variety of examples to illustrate an argument about media/religion/culture.

Ten theoretical explorations of media and religion

Carey, James W. (1992) "A Culture Approach to Communication," *Communication as Culture: Essays on Media and Society*, New York: Routledge.

In this now classic essay Carey argues for a ritual understanding of communication. In contrast to approaches that argue that the task of communication is to reflect a reality outside the communications process, he suggests that reality is not independent of language and argues that reality is brought into existence, produced by human communication, by people's construction, apprehension, and utilization of symbolic forms. Not overtly about religion, Carey's arguments underlie much of the conversation about the way that religion is shaped by its mediation.

Grimes, Ronald L. (2002) "Ritual and the Media," in Hoover, Stewart M. and Lynn Schofield Clark, eds. *Practicing Religion in the Age of the Media: Explorations in Media, Religion, and Culture*, New York: Columbia University Press.

Where Carey argued that communication should be understood as a form of ritual, ritual studies professor Ron Grimes counters that media and ritual are not the same thing. This essay suggests a number of ways in which they interact and reviews the assumptions about ritual in much of the media literature. Grimes particularly questions the view of ritual that suggests it is inherently conservative and tied to the past, and affirms the suggestion that ritual is, or can be, transformative.

Helland, Christopher (2000) "Online-religion/Religion-online and Virtual Communitas," in Hadden, J.K. and D.E. Cowan, eds. *Religion on the Internet: Research Prospects and Promises*, New York: JAI Press.

In this early essay on religion and the Internet Helland makes one of the first attempts to categorize online religious practice. His distinction between *online religion*, where practitioners have high levels of interactivity and a good deal of freedom of voice, and *religion online*, where existing religious authorities provide information but little activity, continues to shape the discussion of the significance of religion in digital spaces. Readers who find this helpful may want to read Helland's later work to see how his thinking, and practice on the Web, has evolved.

Hess, Mary E. (2003) "Practicing Attention in Media Culture," in Mitchell, Jolyon and Sophia Marriage, *Mediating Religion*, Edinburgh: T&T Clark.

Reflecting on her own progressive Roman Catholic community and her teaching in a Protestant seminary, Hess models a media literacy in which faith communities engage the media's presentation of religion (and questions about religion) in ways that deepen their understanding of the challenges and possibilities of religious life in their own cultural context.

Horsfield, Peter (2003) "Electronic Media and the Past-Future of Christianity," in Mitchell, Jolyon and Sophia Marriage, *Mediating Religion*, Edinburgh: T&T Clark.

The author challenges the common assumption that, in the era of electronic and digital media, religion has been deinstitutionalized. Rather, he provocatively suggests that religious faith and practice have been reinstitutionalized within the institutions of commercial mass media. Horsfield argues that, because church leaders have assumed an instrumentalist understanding of the media (i.e. media are simply tools that do not affect the content), they have failed to understand the emerging media cultures. He challenges religious leaders to attend to media as a part of the theological reflection on religion and culture.

Lövheim, Mia and Alf G. Linderman (2005) "Constructing Religious Identity on the Internet," in Højsgaard, Morten and Margrit Warburg, eds. *Religion and Cyberspace,* New York: Routledge.

Two scholars from the Nordic countries, which have seen a striking decline of organized religion and rise in secularity, discuss a range of religious options on the Internet. Traditional forms of religion and new religions are discussed and practiced. While this provides new forms of access, the authors note that the Web is also a location for misinformation and the expression of religious prejudice, and suggest that understanding religion in cyberspace must be part of a full description of religion today.

Meyer, Birgit (2012) "Religious Sensations: Media, Aesthetics, and the Study of Contemporary Religion," in Lynch, Gordon and Jolyon Mitchell with Anna Strahan, eds. *Religion, Media and Culture: A Reader*, London: Routledge.

Drawing upon her own research among Pentecostals in Ghana and other examples, the author deepens the argument that religion cannot be separated from its mediation.

Critiquing definitions of religion that tie it to some pure apprehension of God or the sacred, Meyer demonstrates that religion is rooted in what she calls *sensational forms* that "invoke and organize access to the transcendental." Yet, she resists the suggestion that these experiences should then be understood as fake or inauthentic (p. 160).

Morgan, David (2002) "Protestant Visual Practice and American Mass Culture," in Hoover, Stewart M. and Lynn Schofield Clark, eds. *Practicing Religion in the Age of the Media: Explorations in Media, Religion, and Culture*, New York: Columbia University Press.

Here, as in other works, Morgan lavishly illustrates the argument that for believers the mediations of religion evoke a spiritual presence. In this essay he examines American Protestants' embrace of cheap publishing (tracts, lithography, etc.) as a tool for conversion and character formation. The essay reveals the vibrant visual piety rooted in a domestic religious life practiced by a people who claimed to reject religious images.

Pike, Sarah M. (2008) "Religion," in Morgan, David, ed. *Key Words in Religion, Media and Culture*, New York: Routledge.

The author explores the definition of religion by reflecting on excluded forms of religion. Looking particularly at the interplay of media and Neopagan practices, Pike suggests that the academic study of religion is distorted by scholars' need to categorize some religions as normal and others as deviant. She asks the reader to imagine religion as it is experienced on the margins of society.

Stolow, Jeremy (2005) "Religion and/as Media," *Theory, Culture & Society* 22, no. 4.

This essay advances the argument that religion is best understood as media in careful and critical detail. Stolow challenges the "myth of modern media as agents of secularization." Drawing on examples ranging from Spiritualism and ventriloquism, through the role of media expressions of the tales of the Hindu gods in the rise of Hindu nationalism, to contemporary Christian book burnings and the post-9/11 release of recorded speeches by bin Laden, Stolow engages with the simultaneous privatization of religion and its spread into new public spaces and practices as part of a modern religious project to discipline the senses.

Five provocative case studies

Campbell, Heidi A. (2010) "Studying the Religious Shaping of New Media: The Case of the Kosher Cell Phone," in Campbell, Heidi A., *When Religion Meets New Media*, Abingdon: Routledge.

Rejecting the suggestion that religion is passive and helpless before the inevitable reshaping power of new media, the author examines the way that religious communities reshape technology to serve their religious ends. In this chapter she examines the ultra-Orthodox communities in Israel, who were concerned about the unfettered access to religiously inappropriate and impure information provided by cell phones and the Internet, and the way a kosher cell phone network was developed in response.

Chidester, David (2005) "The Church of Baseball, the Fetish of Coca-Cola, and the Potlatch of Rock and Roll," in Forbes, Bruce David and Jeffrey H. Mahan, eds. *Religion and Popular Culture in America*, Berkeley: University of California Press.

In this playful essay the author discusses three cultural activities or objects that have been argued to be like religion and considers the varied understandings of religion being proposed in these analogies. In doing so, Chidester invites the reader to reflect on what is being mediated in the mediation of religion in popular culture.

Doss, Erica (2002) "Believing in Elvis," in Hoover, Stewart M. and Lynn Schofield Clark, eds. *Practicing Religion in the Age of the Media: Explorations in Media, Religion, and Culture*, New York: Columbia University Press.

Doss makes the case that, through the veneration of Elvis, the establishment of personal and public shrines, and other memorial practices, an Elvis religion, or something quite like a religion, provides a focus for its adherents' reflection and devotion. The essay has served as a model for others who explore the ways that media and popular culture take on the function of religion.

Mitchell, Jolyon (2007) "Toward an Understanding of the Popularity of West African Video Film," in Mitchell Jolyon and S. Brent Plate, eds. *The Religion and Film Reader*, New York: Routledge.

The author examines the rise of an autonomous film industry in Nigeria and Ghana. By studying the videos themselves, their reception by audience members and the self-understanding of actors and producers, Mitchell demonstrates that they are rooted in an African-Pentecostal worldview. He gives attention to the presentation of traditional African religions, demonstrating that they are understood to provide access to real, but malignant, spiritual powers, and that in the films Pentecostal Christianity overcomes these in order to promote an emerging social morality.

Wagner, Rachel (2010) "Our Lady of Persistent Liminality: Virtual Church, Cyberspace, and *Second Life*," in Mazur, Michael and Kate McCarthy, eds. *God in the Details*, 2nd ed., New York: Routledge.

Wagner examines the expression of religion within the online virtual community known as Second Life. People, or at least their avatars, visit detailed reproductions of pilgrimage sites like Mecca or worship spaces from various traditions. Practitioners understand them as virtual sacred spaces. Yet the absence of physical bodies raises questions about certain ritual practices. Orthodox Jewish sites suggest that *minyan* cannot be constituted online, and Christian sites don't offer communion. The author reflects on the liminality of the Second Life space as a location for identity expression and experimentation, and as a location of emerging religious communities.

Index

Taylor & Francis

eBooks

ORDER YOUR FREE 30 DAY INSTITUTIONAL TRIAL TODAY!

FOR LIBRARIES

Over 22,000 eBook titles in the Humanities, Social Sciences, STM and Law from some of the world's leading imprints.

Choose from a range of subject packages or create your own!

- ▶ Free MARC records
- ▶ COUNTER-compliant usage statistics
- ▶ Flexible purchase and pricing options

- ▶ Off-site, anytime access via Athens or referring URL
- ▶ Print or copy pages or chapters
- ▶ Full content search
- ▶ Bookmark, highlight and annotate text
- ▶ Access to thousands of pages of quality research at the click of a button

For more information, pricing enquiries or to order a free trial, contact your local online sales team.

UK and Rest of World: **online.sales@tandf.co.uk**

US, Canada and Latin America: **e-reference@taylorandfrancis.com**

www.ebooksubscriptions.com

Taylor & Francis eBooks
Taylor & Francis Group

A flexible and dynamic resource for teaching, learning and research.

CPSIA information can be obtained
at www.ICGtesting.com
Printed in the USA
BVHW080013120619
550761BV00005B/65/P

9 780415 683203